Motorbooks International

FARM TRACTOR COLOR HISTORY

ORCHARD TRACTORS

Hans Halberstadt

Dedication

For Dave Rogers, our tractor buddy at Case Corporation

We recognize that some words, model names and designations, for example, mentioned herein are the property of the trademark holder. We use them for identification purposes only. This is not an official publication

Motorbooks International books are also available at discounts in bulk quantity for industrial or sales-promotional use. For details write to Special Sales Manager at the Publisher's address

Library of Congress Cataloging-in-Publication Data
Halberstadt, Hans.
  Orchard tractors / Hans Halberstadt.
    p. cm.–(Motorbooks International farm tractor color history)
  Includes index.
  ISBN 0-7603-0141-7 (pbk. : alk. paper)
  1. Farm tractors 2. Fruit–Harvesting–Machinery. I.Title. II. Series.
TL233.6.F37H35 1996   96-18751
629.225–dc20

Printed in Hong Kong

On the front cover: This Massey-Harris 44 is a one-of-a-kind orchard tractor owned by Betty Lamb of Milo, Iowa. Betty's husband Dick purchased the tractor for her after she fell in love with it! The tractor was restored by Dick Carroll.
Frontis: The snappy two-tone paint scheme of the Case 400-series is a bit of a show-stopper. This 1955 400 orchard model belongs to the J.R. Gyger collection and was one of only 80 manufactured with a diesel engine.
Title Page: This was a revolution on wheels, the Oliver Model 70 in orchard dress. It was the first with a 6-cylinder engine. The 70 is often called "the prettiest tractor ever built," and the orchard version is certainly the prettiest of the 70s.
On the back cover: This John Deere AO is one of the "unstyled" versions of the Model AO. It stayed in production from 1935 until 1949. (top) The Cletrac AD "crawler" was a diesel-engined machine, but early crawlers were normally gas-guzzlers until well into the 1930s. (bottom)

CONTENTS

	ACKNOWLEDGMENTS	6
	PREFACE	7
Introduction	TRACTOR IN THE TREES	9
Chapter 1	HISTORY OF THE ORCHARD TRACTOR	29
Chapter 2	WHEELED TRACTORS	39
Chapter 3	CRAWLER TRACTORS	103
	APPENDIX	122
	TRACTOR SPECIFICATIONS	123
	CLUBS, ORGANIZATIONS, AND PUBLICATIONS	127
	INDEX	128

ACKNOWLEDGMENTS

Any book is a team effort but it seems the credit (or blame) goes only to the coach. Well, I'll accept any blame for this but credit should go to the folks who made the book possible. They are the owners, former owners, and historians of these odd, unusual tractors who cooperated in this project. I am grateful to them all.

Augie Scoto
Dick Lamb
Guy Fay
Doug Peltzer
Mike Traill
A. J. "Boots" Kirby
Everett Jensen
Jack Alexander
Irv Baker
Ira Matheny
J. R. Gyger
Dan Schmidt
Jack Cherry, Two-Cylinder Club

Bill Bechtold Sr.
Bill Bechtold Jr.
Tom Graverson
Andrew Lowrey
Lorry Dunning
Jim Becker
Richard Walker
Dean Vinson
Paul Bazetta
K.R. Withrow
Andy Kraushaar

PREFACE

Orchard tractors are a very special, very rare breed; some of the machines shown in this book are the sole survivors of their clan. That makes writing a book about them tremendously enjoyable, and sometimes quite challenging and frustrating. The pleasure comes from the remarkable beauty of these machines; they are quite unlike other tractors in appearance, a consequence of the kind of work these machines were expected to do.

But coming up with reliable, consistent information about these tractors has been very much a hit-and-miss process. Detailed specs for John Deere orchard models are readily available; those for Case orchard models are fragmentary; those for others have evaporated. I even came up with a tractor that worked in an orchard whose manufacturer can't be reliably identified!

So here's the best information I could come up with; when we could find factory specs, I have provided them, and where possible I've tried to compare the orchard model to its standard sibling. Specifications are interesting, and important in books like this, but there is a lot more to the story of a tractor than its overall height or wheelbase. An equally important element of the story ought to be how the machines work in the field, how you start them, hook up an implement, and go to work.

The business of a tractor is *farming*, and we usually leave that out of tractor books. But not in this story. I can't always tell you the names of the engineers and designers who developed these beautiful tractors, so instead I have tried to tell you a different kind of tractor story—the account of how these machines get used in the orchards, and the story of the very exotic and collectable individual restored machines, often in the words of the farmers who *use* these tractors, or who restore and collect them. Where there is information about the evolution of a design, I have included that, too.

Disclaimer:
This kind of book can't include everything about every example of orchard tractor—the nature of the breed makes most of them rare birds and some seem to be completely extinct. We know that some companies, like Ford and Minneapolis-Moline, made some tractors modified for the orchard market, none of which were found during the production of this title. Since very few of these special models were made, and sometimes were little more than custom cosmetic adaptations, there is sometimes no historical information available to the researcher. We've included every scrap of information we could find, and included photos of every make and model in range.

TRACTOR IN THE TREES

*O*ff in the distance, out of sight, the distinctive popping of a tractor materializes. Then, way down at the end of the row of almond trees, a flash of reflected sunlight proclaims the arrival of a glittering green and yellow machine—a John Deere, its steel wheels digging into the sandy soil and propelling it forward. Here comes Irv Baker on his pride and joy AO, through the orchard in full, glorious bloom.

Antique tractors are a big deal these days, and that's good. Americans, on and off the farm, are becoming fascinated with our agricultural heritage. Tractors are a huge part of that heritage, and that fascination—as you will see if you visit any of the hundreds of farm shows, threshing bees, and draft horse "play days" held annually around the country.

You probably won't find many orchard tractors at these events. That's because these extremely beautiful machines are also extremely rare. Few were manufactured and far fewer survive. In some cases only one or two examples exist. But those that have escaped the cutting torch are among the most valuable and sought-after tractors. Collectors search for them, pay substantial prices, and invest tremendous amounts of time and energy in the restoration of these models.

Crawler tractors are extremely common in the groves of the west, Florida, and even parts of the northern midwest. Bill Bechtold, Jr., is disking the winter's cover crop under while the young peach trees in his grove greet the spring with their blossoms.

What Is An "Orchard" Tractor?

Under the sheet metal, orchard tractors are almost always conventional models with swoopy fenders and a low profile. The engines and mechanical components of a John Deere AO are exactly the same as a straight A, but with a lot more sheet metal, a lower seat, and a lower steering wheel. That's pretty much true of all orchard models from all manufacturers, from Case, McCormick-Deering, International Harvester, Minneapolis-Moline, Oliver, Cletrac and Caterpillar. In each case, an orchard model will be a standard model with one or more of the following:

- Oversize fenders to protect trees and fruit from snagging.
- Shrouds and deflectors to protect the operator from impact with limbs.
- Smaller or lower tires to reduce overall height.
- Reduced rear wheel track to allow passage down narrow rows (citrus and vineyard use, primarily).
- Repositioned air intake and engine exhaust from the normal placement on top of the tractor to the underside or back of the machine.
- Lowered seat.
- Lowered steering wheel.

So the story of these orchard models is the story of standard tractors adapted to use in the fruit tree groves of Florida, Michigan, California, Arizona and anywhere commercial fruit production was done on a scale large enough to justify a special model for the market.

Doug Peltzer is safe and sound from the threat of all the thorns on the citrus behind him. A low seat and steering wheel are common features of orchard tractors 'but the heavy shrouds are designed for citrus grove conditions.

The shrouded wheels on Everett Jensen's 1949 Oliver Model 70 Orchard tractor are typical of the beautiful, highly styled machines generally associated with the golden age of tractor design. All that sheet metal is intended to protect the trees from snagging on the tractor as it passes up the rows.

Orchard tractors look different from field and row crop tractors because they work in a different environment with special requirements. Fruit orchards have traditionally needed far more cultivation than other crops. That included frequent discing in the past—"clean cultivation" as the growers call it, to keep the weeds down and the soil "stirred." That has always meant getting in close to the trees, right up to the trunks sometimes, and under the limbs.

But cultivation is just one of the jobs of a tractor in a commercial orchard. Besides plowing and discing, the tractor cuts dikes to control irrigation, rakes up after the annual pruning in the winter, and helps with the harvest by carting bins or specialized picking and harvesting equipment. One of the first applications for the tractor in the orchard was to power spray rigs, first from the pulley and later from the power-take-off (PTO). The commercial fruit orchard is a busy place, pretty much year 'round, and the specialized tractor has been part of the action since about 1910. You can't really appreciate these machines, in spite of their obvious beauty, without an understanding of their mission in life. So let's take a look at the life cycle of an orchard and the work the tractor does during a year.

Working In the Shade

Augie Scoto and his brothers' 2,000 acre diversified operation includes several hundred acres of almonds, marketed through the Sun Diamond cooperative. There are different ways to cultivate an almond orchard, but the Scotos have returned to an old technique that was standard procedure with some growers at the dawn of the tractor age—they plant a cover crop between the rows and practice "no-till" cultivation, mowing when the growth gets too high. The roots of the plants help slow the percolation of irrigation water, allowing more to go to the tree roots. The old method, eighty years ago, was to sow a cover crop in the fall, then plow it under (generally with a horse-drawn disc) in the spring. The idea was that the organic material improved the soil, returned nitrogen and improved tilth, helped

J. R. Gyger's 700-series Case orchard tractor demonstrates the kind of screen and deflector found on many orchard and grove models from the 1950s and 1960s.

retain water during the growing season, and could even be used for pasture. Some farmers endorsed the idea of keeping stock in the orchards, getting a double crop off the same land. This was particularly attractive to poultry operations since chickens needed plenty of green forage material in the summer, and protection from the sun.

Then another method became popular, a "clean tillage" technique that went after every blade of grass anywhere in the grove. Clean-till kept the tractor out in the orchard most months of the year, discing between the rows and back between the trees. "People used to mow and spray to keep the orchard floor perfectly clean," Augie says, "and then we found that the water just disappeared very quickly. We've found that grasses and cover crops make a measurable improvement in yield."

The tillage pattern was very different from what most row crop or grain farmers would find familiar. The traditional clean culture pattern involved discing down the rows of trees, then again between the trees, either at right angles or on the diagonal. Then the farmer pulled a furrow with a plow, irrigating the orchard to the furrow. Then borders were added, with trees planted on 25ft spacings, and the borders controlled the irrigation water.

Tractor Jobs in the Orchard

Although some cover crop is often desirable, and in the west is often allowed to grow all winter, the growth has to be kept under control during the rest of the year. So one of the jobs for the orchard tractor is to make a pass down the rows with a flail mower several times a season. "When the limbs start carrying the crop and begin sagging in the summer and you have to get in there to mow to get ready for the harvest," Augie says, "you've got to get really low to the ground. The tractor has to be very low to the ground to get under those limbs without breaking them or damaging the crop. You really want to avoid hurting the trees!"

Another major tractor job comes when the crop needs to be sprayed—something fruit growers have to do year round. A dormant spray with a simple mineral oil base is applied during the dormant season. This spray isn't a poison but helps control insects *continued on page 15*

Irv Baker lives right smack in the middle of orchard country and he's always looking for interesting old iron, like the nifty early orchard tractor posing in this apricot orchard. This John Deere Model AO is an earlier version than Augie Scoto's shown elsewhere and is equipped with the steel wheels that once were standard equipment on most farm tractors, orchard models or otherwise.

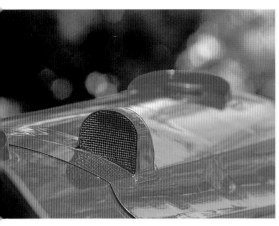

Much thought and effort has been invested in even small details to preclude snags. These are part of an extremely rare and beautiful machine, Betty and Dick Lamb's Massey-Harris 44 Orchard.

The Lindeman-John Deere Model BO tractor was one of many Deere designs that dominated the orchard tractor market. The ground pressure from a conventional tractor compresses the soil, creating irrigation problems. Tracks spread the weight of the machine over a large area, making the pressure far lower. Tracked machines have tremendous advantages for many growers, particularly on hillsides and when the weeds get tall and slick as grease in late winter and early spring.

Right
Spraying is a common chore in many orchards, particularly during winter and spring. One common solution is a simple mineral oil spray that kills larvae by smothering them, rather than poisoning. Another spray is a lime-copper solution used on the fungus spores that create "peach-leaf curl" and other diseases. The sprayers are powered by the PTO of the tractor, and orchard tractors are often equipped with extreme low gears to allow very slow travel through the rows while spraying.

With wheels like those, who needs a cultivator?
The Fageol wasn't welcome on improved
country roads. It took a while for tractor
designers to discover that steel wheels with
cleats like these really didn't improve tractor
efficiency or traction. Rubber tires turned out
to hold better, but it took a couple of decades
for them to displace steel.

BELOW
This bizarre Fageol tractor was another regular
in the orchard. Those spiked wheels were a
1915 invention of Rush Hamilton, from the
apple orchard region around Geyserville,
California. Fageol was based in Oakland, a
center for tractor manufacturing seventy years
ago. This is a 9-12 model, built from 1918
through 1924.

continued from page 11

by suffocating the larvae. Other dormant sprays use sulfur and copper solutions to control fungus diseases that produce peach-leaf-curl, a common problem for stone fruit growers of apricots and peaches. PTO driven sprayers with high-volume fans create a heavy mist that completely saturates each tree with the spray solution.

Late in the year, during the dormant season, most fruit trees are pruned. How heavily depends on the variety of fruit, with stone fruits getting the heaviest attention. The tractor will haul ladders out to the grove for the pruning crew, then come down the rows when the crew is done to clean out the cuttings. A brush rake, front or rear mounted, collects the twigs and limbs and pulls them to the end of the row. Then those piles are pulled together away from the trees and burned. The Scoto brothers use a John Deere 2750 for the purpose, a modern tractor. The current design for the brush rake attaches to the front-end loader. With this system you push the prunings ahead of the tractor. An earlier design attached to the rear of the tractor on the three-point-hitch, somewhat like a hayrake.

"Avoiding the limbs is the major problem in the grove," according to Augie. "People have been knocked off the seat and lost eyes from hitting the tree limbs, so safety is one of the important considerations in orchard tractor design. A tall row-crop tractor just won't work in an orchard. For one thing, the muffler is always in the wrong place for use in the trees. An orchard tractor always has the muffler on the side or underneath, otherwise it would quickly break off! A real orchard tractor is designed to be able to work under the trees without breaking anything on the tractor or the tree itself."

In the early days of orchard tractors, and up until fairly recently, one use for the machine was to carry the picking tarps through the grove. These tarps attached to long trailers and the fabric was cut to fit around the trunk of the tree, covering the ground around the base. The pickers came along with heavy mallets, and when they hammered on the trunk of the tree, the nuts all fell on the tarp. The pickers then could easily roll the tarp up, depositing the nuts up into the wagon.

A Year In the Orchard

An orchard tractor really gets a workout. It is out in the grove all the time, year round, helping with all the chores. Starting with winter (November through January in California's central valley) that begins with cleaning the trees of "mummies," the fruit that didn't fall from the tree. We go out in the rows with fiberglass poles and do it by hand, but the tractor comes along behind to clean up the ground.

Late in January we use the orchard tractor to spray the borders of the grove with herbicide, but we don't plow as some growers do. We sometimes have to spray the trees in winter to control "twig borer," and egg mites.

We bring in the bee hives in late January or early February, just before the bloom usually begins.

And in February or March we'll have to spray about that time, too, with a "bloom spray" — that's what we use to control scale insects.

As soon as it gets dry enough, we'll go in and mow the grass to keep it under control. That will happen in March or early April. At "petal fall" we always worry about frost — that's a critical time. We always mow real close at that time because the tall grass seems to attract the frost.

Then, toward the end of April, we get ready to start irrigating. This is also the time we start applying fertilizer.

As summer begins we continue to monitor the weeds closely, check plant nutrients, and watch for summer mites. These little insects can make the leaves fall off the trees, and we sometimes have to spray to control them.

Toward the end of summer we have to watch for hull-splitting and naval orange worm. Those indicate more spraying.

Then it is time to get ready for the harvest. We spray the floor of the orchard with Round Up; this kills off all the grass for a few weeks and leaves a perfectly clean floor for the harvest. Then we go in and start shaking the trees and collecting the nuts.

After the harvest we go back in with another application of nitrogen just before the dormant season begins. And this is also the time, in late Fall, when we take out any trees that are sick or dead, to be replanted during the winter.

Then we prune and push the brush out with the brush rake toward the end of November or beginning of December.

Augie Scoto, Scoto Brothers Orchards

Citrus Cultivation

Citrus trees need very different care from that required for apples, apricots, and other fruits grown in cold winter climate areas of the country. Citrus culture has changed a bit over the years, and that has changed the shape of orchard tractors. Here's how Doug Peltzer's family has been doing things:

Normal cultivation of citrus back in the 1930s and 1940s started in the spring with discing the weeds down, leveling the ground, followed by cross-furrowing with a tool with about six shovels. Then the tractor was used to put in ridges with blocks to control the irrigation water by conveying the water between the tree rows, flowing across the cross-furrows to each tree. The farmer could expect to irrigate three times after each cultivation before the process had to be repeated. "There would typically be four or five of these cultivation-irrigation cycles per year," Doug Peltzer recalls.

Discing citrus groves was the only alternative for weed control before selective herbicides became available about fifty years ago. Weeds like wild mustard can take over a grove in just a few weeks, filling in the rows with solid growth that Doug Peltzer has measured at 15ft. Once the weeds get established they are hard to disc under and can even make navigation a problem for the tractor operator. "I recall one year, after a pro-*continued on page 18*

Smooth steel wheels like these had real advantages in the orchard. Unlike the spoked variety, common on some designs, the smooth wheel didn't snag branches sagging close to the ground under the burden of a heavy crop.

RIGHT
The Fageol uses a Lycoming 4-cylinder engine with 3.5in by 5in bore and stroke, a Tillotson carb and Dixie magneto. It weighs about 3,600lb and cost $1,525. This rare example is part of the extensive Antique Gas & Steam Engine Museum collection at Vista, California, just north of San Diego.

continued from page 15

longed winter, we had to disc three times and the first time the disc never actually touched the ground, the weeds were so thick! When I was a kid," Doug says, "discs used to be fairly small—about 7ft wide, with blades that started at 18in. Today, we start with 26in blades and discard them at 16in. I have disced when the weeds were so big that I couldn't see ahead, the only way to steer was by watching the trees on my left side, using them as a guide. This was on mildly rolling hills, too, and the vegetation was so slick that the Caterpillar was loosing traction. This work would have been totally impossible with a wheeled tractor."

"We farm on some hillsides that are relatively steep and a crawler is just far safer from roll-over. Also, on a side slope, a wheeled tractor will have one wheel pulling and the other won't—you can't use differential lock and keep the tractor going straight down the row. That's just not a problem with a crawler! I have had crawlers slide off a hill, but you just slide—not roll."

Tillage practices and tractor use in citrus groves are radically different today than 40 to 50 years ago, before herbicides were available. Growers want a "clean" floor to the orchard, summer and winter. In the winter that means a clean orchard that is two or three degrees warmer than one with a cover crop—a critical consideration. Doug Peltzer says, "Citrus growers are extremely concerned about frost damage, and those two or

Desperate men take desperate measures. This kind of tire prevents blowouts from lemon tree thorns, a chronic problem for the growers who raise citrus. The thorns harden into 1.5in spikes, guaranteed to puncture any conventional tire working the groves sooner or later, even the 22-ply versions used on many orchard tractors.

Orchard tractors intended for use in orange and lemon groves are generally enclosed in huge, swoopy fenders. This John Deere unstyled A Orchard demonstrates how they work, and how they are damaged, by the trees in the orchard. Low, close growth is particularly common in citrus groves like this stand of Valencia oranges.

three degrees can make an important difference in your crop on a cold night. Then, too, almost all citrus in California and the west needs irrigation; water is expensive and if you grow a cover crop you've got to supply it with water, a costly item."

Cover crops were grown then, too, either seeded or allowed to grow naturally, then disced under to provide organic material and help with water retention.

"Today we disc to reestablish ground contour to help with water flow. There are lots of theories about what discing does to the soil and water retention, but what we've found is that you can disc regularly to four inches and have nice, mulchy soil that you think will have excellent penetration. Under that four inches, though, can be a four inch "plow sole" that you've created by going over the ground with your tractor. Like hardpan, it keeps the water from getting to the trees. We've found in those cases we can't cure the problem with discing, but by using organic material and breaking up the "plow sole" with a "subsoiler" tool in extreme cases. In some cases we've had to take a large D8 Caterpillar into an established orchard to rip up the ground. A certain amount of root-pruning results, but it has been necessary to revitalize the trees."

Ira Matheney's McCormick-Deering Model W-30 Orchard is a barn-fresh example of a pretty rare machine. It runs, is mostly complete, and will keep Ira busy for a while. This is a good example of the second generation of orchard tractors, in its natural environment. This photograph was made three weeks after the tractor emerged from a 25-year sleep in a shed where it had been parked for the last time after retirement. Although never cranked in all that time, Ira cleaned out the mouse nests, added some fresh gas, and gave the crank a twirl—it fired up.

Normal row spacing in citrus today is about 22ft, although some growers will plant to as much as 28ft or as little as 14ft. Left unpruned, citrus will grow together into a giant hedge, taking over the rows. That habit of growth is the reason for those big "grove" or "citrus" fenders; before power hedging units came on the market the trees filled out more than they are allowed to today. "We prune for between six- and eight-foot clearance today," Doug reports.

22-Ply Tires?

Citrus may give you a crop year round, but it gives you problems year round, too. One of these problems is particularly apparent if you take a conventional tractor into a lemon grove. Within a few acres or so, all the tires will be flat. Lemons and oranges both produce thorns but the ones on orange trees are small and not very dangerous; lemons, however, are a different story. The thorns on a lemon tree grow to about an inch and a half, sometimes longer. When a twig or branch gets knocked to the ground the thorns harden into very sharp, hard little spikes. A thorn will punch right through a six-ply tire with ease. Grove tractors and hedging units use 22-ply tires to defeat them, but even these remarkably thick casings only last a couple of years before they go flat, too. That's another reason for using crawler tractors in citrus—the tracks are steel and they're already flat!

Doug Peltzer's family has owned and used this McCormick-Deering since it was new, back in the 1920s. The Peltzer clan raised citrus in the Anaheim, California, area back when it was still rural. The family now operates a 2,000-acre grove operation near Porterville, California.

Citrus is harvested every month of the year on the Peltzer farm, and Doug eats some of the product every day. It doesn't get much fresher than this, and it doesn't get much more fun than to putt around the rows on one of your old John Deere tractors; this is a Model 620.

Augie Scoto is a young lad in his 30s but he and his brothers have built the family farm from 300 acres to 2,000. It is a diversified operation, including walnuts, almonds, tomatoes, alfalfa, and some corn. Here he's disking some new trees with his handsome John Deere Model AO. Disking was once a very common orchard chore but is less used today; no-till cultivation is standard in most orchards, including groves of mature trees on the Scoto place.

Augie Scoto's John Deere AO in a mature grove of almond trees on the "home place." The Scotos practice "no-till" cultivation in the groves, allowing a cover crop to grow between the rows, mowing it back rather than plowing it under when it gets too big. The tractor is a 1948 machine, shipped originally to San Jose, California, and used for many years in the vast fruit groves of the California Central Valley. Augie found it in a shed, a basket case, with ivy growing up through the engine.

Growers still need tractors in the groves and here comes a modern example of the breed. It is a John Deere Model 2355, chopped and lowered and with custom fenders and exhaust, low profile tires, and a job to do at sunrise on this crisp April morning in an apricot orchard in full bloom.

LEFT
Disking under the cover crop and keeping the orchard floor clean and sterile was once accepted practice when the 530 model from Case came out. *J. I. Case*

There is a lot of work for a tractor in an orchard, and the J. I. Case Co. offered the 530 for work like this, mowing down the grass, weeds, or cover crop between the rows. *J. I. Case*

Richard Walker uses his restored Caterpillar Model 22 and a disk furrowing tool to prepare his citrus grove for irrigation. The three-point-hitch is an elegant, home-engineered fabrication that took about as much time to make as the tractor restoration required. *Richard Walker*

Richard Walker in his 1935 Cat 22, using a spring-tooth harrow to groom the orchard floor. *Richard Walker*

CHAPTER 1

A BRIEF HISTORY OF THE ORCHARD TRACTOR

*T*he American farmer's love affair with the tractor started over 100 years ago, during the 1880s when practical steam "traction engines" started appearing on farms all over the country. The steamer has many virtues and rapidly displaced horses as a source of motive power on big grain operations in the west, and as a stationary power source all over the country. Steamers did a lot of important work—but just about none of it in the orchard. The smallest of the breed was just too big to fit!

The gasoline engine was invented in the 1880s, developed in the 1890s, and pretty well perfected by 1900 when thousands of little gas buggies and early trucks were already putting around America. A gasoline engine has some very important virtues: it is light and very powerful for its weight, and very compact. Its fuel is also quite compact, particularly when compared to the wood and coal and water a steamer needs to produce the same amount of power. It wouldn't blow up, as a steamer did somewhere in America every day back then, and a little gas tractor didn't need a special engineer or fireman to keep it in action. Even with the early, experimental models, the gasoline engine was an

Difficult footing in the soft ground typically found in orchards makes tracks a natural form of traction. The drive train on this machine includes simple clutch and transmission, a short shaft and a large drive wheel.

exciting development in the mechanization of the farm, and for the rest of America, too.

So what was the first gasoline-powered farm tractor? That seems to depend on who you ask. One version gives credit to the Waterloo Gasoline Traction Engine Company with an 1892 design. This tractor, designed and built by John Froelich, was based on a Robinson steam tractor chassis and drive train, but with power supplied by a Van Duzen four-stroke-cycle gas engine. It looked a lot like a stationary gas engine bolted to a small steam engine chassis, for good reason.

This prototype conversion worked well enough to complete a threshing run that year. The converted tractor moved a threshing machine from one farm to the next, threshing grain at each, cleaning about 72,000 bushels

continued on page 32

The J.I Case Company made lots of orchard tractors over the years, including the DO shown puttering off for a rub-down at J.R. Gyger's retirement community for old tractors. J.R. and his kids provide nothing but the best in accommodations for a selected group of historically important examples of the tractor designers' art, with a special emphasis on grove and orchard veterans.

Here's one of the first-ever orchard tractors, saved from the scrap pile. It is *probably* a Bean Track-Pull from about 1915, but there isn't a mark on it anywhere. This layout was patented by Sunnyvale, California, designer Alf Johnson; it may be a prototype of his, but owner Bill Traill is mystified. The machine came out of a Santa Clara, California, county orchard and went to a junk yard; the scrap dealer—bless him—saved it and sold it to a tractor collector. Although it hasn't run for a year or two, the engine produces an occasional pop, and Bill has hopes for his new machine.

RIGHT
A beefy two-cylinder engine provides the go-power. Eighty years ago tractor designers didn't always worry about shrouds and shields and other safety items. You were expected to keep your fingers out of the fan, and if you didn't the resultant damage was your own fault.

LEFT
The cockpit of this early orchard machine is brutally simple: steering wheel, clutch control, and throttle is all you get. This was a typical layout for early tractors of all kinds. Although simple, the construction is sturdy and well designed, and built for eternity.

continued from page 29

during the season. Based on that performance, Froelich built four new machines for sale. Two sold but were returned when the farmers—understandably—couldn't figure out how to keep them working. So that is one version of the first farm tractor.

The *generally* accepted claim for the first *production* tractor with a gasoline engine appeared in 1902, at Charles City, Iowa, the legendary Hart-Parr. There are several other versions of the story, with others claiming priority and other dates mentioned, but this is the one the Smithsonian Institution credits as the first real gasoline powered tractor. The Hart-Parr was strictly a field tractor, though. It was as big and heavy as a steamer and if you drove it through most orchards the trees would look like stubble.

It wasn't long until quite a few competitors entered the tractor market and a real cat fight developed. These tractors looked like steamers, used steamer parts, and weighed as much as steamers—up to fifteen tons, in some cases. They even broke through bridges just like steamers.

Although early gas tractors looked a lot like steamers, and were just about as bulky, compact models started coming on the market before 1910. These little machines could sometimes beat the big steamers—and keeping them going was much easier and more economical than in the past.

As a result, a tremendous boom in tractor production occurred. You could sell anything that had an engine in it and someplace to hook a plow, no questions asked. The market was quickly flooded by machines that some-

times worked, sometimes didn't. By 1915, over 500 companies in the United States were building and selling tractors, some as a sideline, others as a principal business. But very few specialized in machines specifically intended for the orchard. However, starting about 1917 the whole tractor market started to sort itself out—and fruit growers finally started to find models that worked in between the trees. These tractors were almost always standard field machines designed for wide open spaces but some were found that could maneuver in the tight quarters of the standard orchard.

To exploit this market niche, manufacturers promoted almost anything. In 1912 Avery promoted its 12-25, one of its smallest models, for the fruit growers' market even though the machine stood 10ft tall. But the machine cultivated well enough to get this

Somewhat similar machines appear in the Bean Spray Pump Company's tractor catalogue in the World War I era, but with bigger engines and other modifications that make owner Bill Traill suspect this is a Johnson prototype. Bean, a San Jose, California, company, was a major supplier of orchard equipment early in the century and sold a line of similar tractors for orchard use. The company was later sucked up into the giant Food Machinery Company (FMC). A very few similar Bean "Track Pull" tractors have been preserved; the company produced them until 1920.

The Waterloo Boy was the first tractor to wear the John Deere name, but not its first design—that came later. When John Deere finally decided to get into the tractor market, after much careful consideration, hundreds of other manufacturers were already there. Deere jumped in by purchasing one, the Waterloo Gasoline Engine Company, and their product, the *Waterloo Boy*. It turned out to be a wise choice; the tractor was quite popular, sold well, and was the first of the long line of green machines. It was used in many orchards and there is evidence, according to Jack Cherry of the Two-Cylinder Club, of a "California Special" version modified specially for orchard use, but none are known to definitely exist—although rumors of one have circulated for years.

testimonial from the Director of the Missouri Fruit Experiment Station, Paul Evans. He said, "where peach trees under ordinary conditions made a growth of only a few inches during the season on account of drought, and where the fruit was not much more than one-half the size it should be, orchards cultivated with the tractors produced an immense crop of fruit of good size and eight year old trees made an average growth in addition to maturing this crop of

something like two feet. We have arranged to dispose of the greater part of our horses and mules and expect to use tractors exclusively for the cultivation of our orchards."

In response to the demand for suitable tractors, manufacturers built and promoted small, comparatively light machines and promoted them to the orchard trade. Avery introduced an even smaller model, the 8-16. This tractor, at only 52in high and 56in wide, actually started to fit the job. The 12-25 used

by the Missouri Experiment Station weighed in at 7,500lb; the little 8-16 was a lightweight at only 4,600lb. This machine didn't use a fan, fuel pump, or water pump, turned on a dime, and could get under the trees—or so Avery salesmen liked to claim; actually, you can't get a kiddy car under the loaded limbs of many orchards late in the season, and not under citrus trees any time of the year.

But farmers were abuzz with the very idea of doing their cultivation with tractors instead of horses, and here was the recommended technique in 1912.

Fred Chadborne started using tractors on the 250 acres of his Suisun Valley, California, orchard during the 1908 season. He used a Johnson tractor, an odd-looking machine with chain drive and tricycle layout. The Johnson was made in Sunnyvale, California, in what is now downtown "Silicon Valley" but back then it and all of Santa Clara County was one of the major fruit growing regions of the United States. The Johnson cost $1,750 in 1910, a hefty sum, and claimed to cultivate an acre an hour with a four-bottom plow. According to their ads (not a reliable source of performance data back then) the Johnson generated 30hp and used three gallons of distillate fuel per hour.

Chadborne was experimenting with the machine. The Johnson was a new machine—a new kind of machine, used in a new way. So he started with his existing tillage tools, horse plows with five 24in discs, altered for the tractor's hitch. Because of the size of his operation, Chadborne bought two of the Johnson tractors, augmented with a team of horses cutting furrows between alternate rows of trees.

He pulled them at 2.5mph, turning a 48in swath. Chadborne discovered that he spent, on average, $4.25 per day for the tractors working the orchard. Each consumed 25 gallons of distillate at eight cents per gallon, and twenty five cents worth of lube oil; the rest of the money was for the operator since Chadborne didn't try to calculate repairs or depreciation for his little test. He was able to cultivate about fifteen acres per day in this manner.

After the plowing, he used an 11ft "crosskill" roller on one tractor, followed by the second and a cultivator. A "duckfoot" cultivator provided maintenance cultivation later in the season, as required.

By 1913 the Holt Manufacturing Company, close to both the Chadborne farm in Suisun and the extensive groves in Santa Clara County, was already pushing its Baby Caterpillar for orchard work. "Turns in its own length! Won't bark the trees," Holt proclaimed and both were important considerations for orchard owners considering a tractor.

By 1915 the concept had been pretty well validated and industry experts were promoting the conversion to tractors from

Sheet metal shrouds and fenders were first improvised, then made standard equipment for tractors marketed to the orchard industry. The size and shape of these fenders varied a bit with the intended use, but the biggest (like these) were normally intended for the citrus industry and its low-hanging branches. This lovely machine is Betty Lamb's Massey Harris 44 Orchard.

Oliver 70 Orchard tractor disking a Florida citrus grove, circa 1935. *Oliver—Hart-Parr Archives, Floyd County Museum, Charles City, Iowa*

horses and mules. A 1915 report on citrus production advised,

The availability in California of large quantities of cheap fuel oils has made possible a great increase in the use of orchard tractors. There are a number of these machines now on the market, some of which have proven economical and satisfactory. While the mule is by far the most flexible motor for small jobs and for work on broken ground such s contour plantings, the tractor is gradually displacing the mule on large tracts of level land. A grower

who keeps sixteen head of mules worth $2,400 may retain four or five for light work and with the money from the sale of the others get a machine that will do the work of the original sixteen. The engineering of such a machine appeals much more to the average farm boy than hitching, unhitching, and feeding the mules, morning, noon, and night! The tractor is also immune to the high heat of the interior valleys, which is often embarrassing to work-stock. With a tractor it is possible to till a larger proportion of the orchard area at the right time.

The work in citrus orchards demands a low down, light, short-turning gas tractor either of the three wheel or caterpillar type. The machine should not exceed five feet in height and should be provided with steel hood or limb protector. Extra strong tillage implements must be used with tractors, as otherwise serious breakage may result when stones or stumps are struck. An ordinarily good orchard tractor should plow about twelve acres of orchard a day at a cost, including an ample allowance for interest and depreciation, of not over $12.40

Oliver 70 with spray rig, circa 1935. *Oliver—Hart-Parr Archives, Floyd County Museum, Charles City, Iowa*

Factory rendering of the Oliver 77 Orchard tractor. *Oliver—Hart-Parr Archives, Floyd County Museum, Charles City, Iowa*

The platform of this Oliver 70-series orchard tractor offers more room and operator protection than did many competing machines, one reason why the Oliver 70 was such a popular machine. *Oliver—Hart-Parr Archives, Floyd County Museum, Charles City, Iowa*

CHAPTER 2

WHEELED TRACTORS

DEERE & COMPANY

*J*ohn Deere is one of the oldest American companies in continuous operation, nearly 160 years at this writing. It began in 1837 when its namesake, a blacksmith, developed a plow that was clearly superior to the competition. For many years the Deere company furnished tillage tools to the American farmer—walking plows, sulky plows, harrows, planters; then the line was expanded to include harvesting machinery—mowers in particular, and binders later. The company was one of many "long line" vendors serving the American farmer at the time, and survived many shakeouts by sticking to its corporate foundation and not trying (as the Case company did) to design and build threshers, steam engines, tillage tools, and everything else.

But the big tractor market that quickly developed around 1915 got the company interested. Instead of developing a new model, in 1918 Deere bought an existing company with a proven product. The company was Waterloo Gasoline Engine Co. and the product was the *Waterloo Boy* tractor-the first of a very illustrious family.

Deere is the proverbial 800lb gorilla in the tractor industry, past and present, and its orchard models are the most common exam-

John Deere's Model GP (for "General Purpose") entered the market in 1928, the GPO orchard version in 1931. Like the rest of the line for many years, the heart of the beast was the horizontal 2-cyliner engine Deere inherited with the Waterloo Boy. This example belongs to Doug Peltzer, part of an almost complete set of John Deere orchard tractors.

Augie Scoto likes to take the AO out for a spin once in a while, and what could be more fun than a trip around the trees with a big disk, combining some business with pleasure. While it is always nice to see a restored tractor at a show, it is more fun to watch one work.

ples of the breed you'll find at shows. Deere is still providing orchard tractors to the American fruit grower, the collectables of the future. Here's a thumbnail history of Deere's general purpose tractor lineup:

JOHN DEERE
Grove and Orchard Tractors

And a Complete Line of Orchard Equipment

For Groves, Orchards, Vineyards, and Hopyards

Waterloo Boy

The Waterloo Boy was the first real John Deere tractor, and many certainly saw service in orchards and groves even if they weren't sold specifically for that purpose. It was a compact, tight-turning, early tractor, but a practical design that made quite a hit on the market when Deere brought it out just after World War I. The Waterloo Boy was the first to be tested in the famous Nebraska Tractor Tests, in 1920.

The Waterloo Boy's foundation was a large two-cylinder engine with a 6.5in bore and 7in stroke that at 750rpm powered the tractor to twelve drawbar horsepower and twenty five on the pulley. Actually, the Nebraska test found it did a bit better, almost 16hp at the drawbar and just over twenty five brake horsepower. The Waterloo Boy's best effort produced a pull of 2,900lb on the dyno at a speed of 2.07mph. The tractor consumed 3.8gal of kerosene per hour, or 6.83 horse-

LEFT
Brochure cover for John Deere Orchard products from the 1930s. *John Deere*

Although the air intake and exhaust have been repositioned, the radiator screened, and a little sheet metal added to cover those big steel wheels, there are still enough places on the Model GPO to snag the trees in the grove while driving up and down the rows. *John Deere*

While hardly tricked out with all the "custom" stuff on later orchard designs, the GPO at least had a screen over the radiator and the air intake and exhaust plumbing routed low, out of the way. Cooling was with what Deere called the "thermo-siphon" system that re-circulated coolant without benefit of a water pump.

power-hours per gallon. It had two forward speeds—slow, and slower. The test engineers faulted the tractor for a governor that didn't govern very well, but not so badly that the machine could not be sold in Nebraska. It was the first of many to pass the Nebraska tests. Deere's intention was, at first, to quickly

phase out the old Waterloo Boy tractor but farmers kept buying the tractors for years, the last going out the door in 1924.

Jack Cherry, a thirty- year employee of the Deere company and member of the Two Cylinder Club, says, "If you're going to talk about John Deere orchard tractors, you

really have to go way back to the beginning, to the Waterloo Boy and start there. Not many people know this, but there was an orchard version of this machine called the California Special. They shortened the wheelbase and used a single front wheel. There is a drawing of this tractor showing

JOHN DEERE
Models "AO" and "BO"
GROVE and ORCHARD TRACTORS

When you buy John Deere Implements you are sure of prompt repair service during their long life.

Brochure cover for the AO and BO line, circa 1940. *John Deere*

Owners Will Tell You --

Owners will tell you that a fully tricked out AOS like the one on this brochure cover is a nice addition to your collection, and much too valuable to allow to play in the dirt. *John Deere*

the wheel mounted forward on an early unit, and another record of one with the front wheel mounted farther back, about a foot or so; that would have made for a tighter turning radius that would have been needed in the orchard. We have found some reference to these in the Deere archives, in the Waterloo Boy serial number register. There are rumors of one of these California Specials somewhere out there—an *extremely* rare machine, if it exists."

Model D

Deere bought the Waterloo company to have tractors to sell, and a factory to build tractors, but set to work immediately to design something better of its own. Deere succeeded spectacularly with the John Deere Model D, a

product that stayed in the showroom for more than thirty years. This simple, economical, durable tractor offered 15hp at the drawbar, 27hp at the pulley at the beginning of its long life, and more as the years went by.

The D was never offered as an orchard variant but saw extensive use in commercial fruit operations all over the country. The Deere factory attempted to develop its own crawler tractor in the early thirties, an experimental program that produced about ten machines with the designation *Model D Crawler*. The D was introduced in 1924 and lasted until 1953.

"The D was never adapted to an orchard model," Jack says, "it was too big and too clumsy to get around in the orchard very well. Even so, Deere offered some equipment

for orchard use for the D because of customer demand—Deere always responded well to customer demand. These were modifications that changed the position of the muffler and covered the wheels to protect citrus, little things like that. A few Ds were made with tracks but these were not intended for orchard use, but for increased traction; they were tested only in Montana and properly called Model D—Crawler-Type in the records."

Model GP

Deere's GP (for "General Purpose") came on the market in 1928, at the end of a long period of depressed farm prices and extremely difficult market conditions for vendors of plows, tractors, and harvesting

Deere didn't bother re-plumbing the AO's intake and exhaust, they just cut them off and covered them up with rounded castings.

Augie Scoto's 1949 John Deere Model AO poses in front of one of the machinery sheds on the home place. By the time this AO was built rubber tires were pretty much the norm, displacing the steel versions that had been standard equipment during most of the first half of the century.

equipment. The new GP was introduced to go head to head with industry giant International Harvestor.

The GP was rated initially as a 10-20 tractor, producing 10hp at the drawbar, 20hp at the pulley. In its wide tread configuration the GP had plenty of clearance for corn and other row crops requiring cultivation. The GP introduced power-lift for plows and discs, an industry first. Within a few years the engine was up-rated to about fifteen drawbar horsepower, about 24hp on the pulley.

Deere, along with many manufacturers at the time, hedged its bets with power specifications. Rather than claim a figure that might be refuted by the Nebraska tests, they simply said the machine was "suitable for two 14in plows or 22in thresher or 24in John Deere thresher." The distillate engine GP was tested in May of 1931, producing 25.36hp at the pulley and 18.86 at the drawbar.

Most of the GP series used engines with 6in bore and stroke, rated for 950rpm. These engines used magneto ignition with an impulse starter. Lubrication was pressurized but the cooling system used a passive "thermo-siphon" design that avoided a water

pump. The tranny offered your choice of three forward speeds and a head-snapping 4mph at redline. With tanks dry the little tractor weighed in at just over two tons. The basic GP stayed in production for eight years, from 1928 to 1935. The GP was adapted for orchard use and the new modified model was called the GPO.

GPO

Deere's entry into the market for orchard-specific tractors was the GPO, introduced in April of 1931 with the uprated engine. Production lasted for four years, ending in 1935 with 711 units produced. Some of these were converted to crawlers by Lindeman Power Equipment Company of Yakima, Washington, and eleven GP crawlers still survive.

Deere promoted the GPO heavily, proclaiming the virtues of its heavy two-cylinder engine. Sturdiness is built into every part of the engine to give maximum service in heavy-duty work, they said. For example, the crankshaft is 3in in diameter. Only two main bearings are required. These are extra wide, 3.5in, and only a short distance apart, 13.5in. There is no springing of the crankshaft under heavy loads.

Okay, is this cute or what? A clean and tidy John Deere Model BO ventures out into the citrus for a look around. The basic B model was a good foundation for an orchard tractor; it was small, low, and didn't have a lot of unnecessary pep.

John Deere AO driver's console. The instrumentation is rather Spartan, the controls not quite ergonomic, the air-conditioning a faint, fond hope, but this tractor helped grow an awful lot of fruit. Differential brakes help with the turns at the end of the row, and a hydraulic lift made raising and lowering the implement a lot easier than with earlier tractors.

The zap for this BO comes from a Fairbanks Morse magneto, the heart of the tractor's simple little ignition system.

It really was a cute little thing. The seat position was extra low, reducing the risk to the driver of impact with limbs and branches. The GP wasn't the longest-lasting design, or Deere's most popular, but it set the stage for similar versions soon to come. There aren't a lot of those 711 GPOs still around but the ones that are, like Doug Peltzer's, are lovingly cared for as an important bit of farm history—Chapter One in the long saga of John Deere orchard tractors.

Doug Peltzer's GPO has a sad history. It sold originally in 1934 to a citrus grower in Farmersville, California. Sometime not long after, the tractor was driven across railroad tracks ahead of a train—almost. A collision occurred and the operator was killed. After that, the GPO was rebuilt but used as a stationary power source for a sawmill. Doug acquired it recently and added it to his almost complete set of Deere orchards.

According to Jack Cherry, "Lindeman developed the first GPO, based on a 1929 GP. My dad and Fred Heilmann drove out there to look at the thing and came back to convince the company that we ought to produce it. The factory shipped a GP out there to Yakima where the Lindeman people chopped it up, added pieces to the fender, changed the front axle, dropped the tractor, all in an experiment to see if it would work in an orchard setting. Deere introduced it in 1932, with serial numbers 15000, and on. That's important to know if you get interested in these early Deere orchard models. These early GPOs were built from left-over GP Wide Tread tractors, of all things! These machines were sitting around the Waterloo factory as unsold inventory because they had odd-ball engines with 5.75in bores instead of the 6in used on the rest of the line. The first six GPO tractors were built from wide-tread machines with a goofy "cross-over" intake manifold—and they are numbered 14994 through 14999. Walt Keller has one of these, and these six are key examples—the very first orchard models made by Deere, the foundation for the whole long line of Deere orchard tractors."

Model A

Deere's all-time best seller has been the Model A, produced from 1934 to 1952. Nearly a third of a million were built over those eighteen years. The price for the tractor varied considerably over that time, but the last ones cost about $2,400.

The design of the A changed many times, with increased power, new features, and then "styling." Engine displacement increased from 309ci to 321ci, and power output grew to match, from about 16hp to 19hp to 34hp—not bad for a simple, solid two-banger chugging away at a rated 975rpm. The transmission, originally four speeds forward, became a six-speed. The A got stretched as well as buffed, growing from 124in overall to 134in. The A offered hydraulic lift, differential brakes (highly useful in an orchard) and adjustable rear-wheel tread.

Jack Cherry on Deere Orchard Models

The lineage for John Deere's orchard models is a little difficult to follow, but here it is: the AO continued from 1949 to 1953 with standard or citrus fenders, and engine guards, if you wanted; this is a very pretty tractor!

The B stopped at 1947 without ever being styled.

Then came the Model 50—but no orchard versions of the 50 were made. None of its offspring, the 520, or the 530, were adapted for orchard use either. Well, let's get on the other side of the Model A and talk about the G—it was never an orchard either. The 70, 720, and 730 didn't get the treatment. Then go one step further, to the Model R, 80, 820, 830—but none of these were made into an orchard tractor. Finally, the Model 60 was adapted to an orchard model; it rolled over into a 620 Orchard, and it stayed in the line all the way up to 1960. It might have been converted to the 630 version, but Deere didn't bother. The difference between the 20-series to the 30-series involved small improvements of seat position, control convenience, comfort, but with the same powerplant and drive train. The orchard model already had a lower seat in the 620 so there wasn't much to change. That's the end of the two-cylinder story in John Deere orchard tractors.

Shortly after the machine was introduced as the "AS" (for Model A Standard) it was renamed the "AR" (for Model A Regular), then it was rechristened yet again as the Model A (Standard Tread). Jack Cherry, who has studied this machine in detail, says, "I think it was dropped in anticipation of having a Model B Standard Tread—and I think

they didn't want to call it the 'BS!' Deere made the tractor as an AR, the regular tread model, the AO orchard model, and industrial model called the AI."

John Deere Model AO – 1935 to 1953

There were several variations on the AO theme, the first appearing in 1935—and this can get a little confusing. There were three sets of AO tractors, all from John Deere. One was the AO *unstyled* that was offered from 1935 to 1940, then changed slightly and produced from 1940 to 1949. A second AO, the Streamlined or AOS, was not offered concurrently with the unstyled AO from 1936 to 1940. A third AO appeared in 1949, with the styling treatment and all the modern amenities.

All of these were AOs, although they could look like three different designs. It was complicated by the decision by Deere to have Henry Dryfus style the AR in 1939, then wait ten years to do the same thing to the AO variant. From 1949 to 1953 you could get the stylish AO with regular fenders or optional citrus fenders, or engine guards. It was a very pretty tractor either way.

Just as the A was an updated version of the GP, the AO was a revised GPO with essentially the same power and similar dimensions. This first AO was built in 1935 and suspended from production in early October 1936, to be

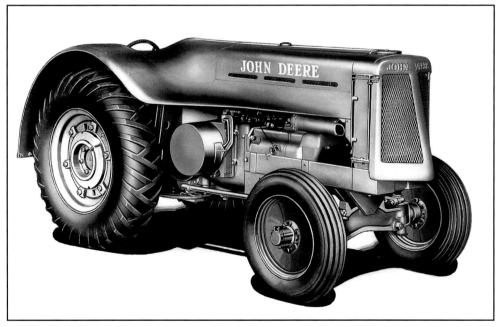

This is the "Streamlined" AO, the Model AOS, offered concurrently with the unstyled Model AO from 1936 to 1940. *John Deere*

The John Deere Model BO was never styled during its long production run, but farmers liked the basic lines of the B well enough to buy about 300,000 of them in all. Only about 5,300 of the orchard model were built, though, making it one of the more exotic green machines around.

replaced by the AOS. These machines stayed in production until the end of October 1940. The last AOs came out of the factory in 1953, the end of a very long era. During that long run a total of 2,687 orchard models of the basic A were built in several variations. The orchard version was five inches shorter, at 55in to the top of the radiator cap, than the standard A, and weighed in a bit heavier at 4,088lb.

The last Nebraska test for the A began on June 7, 1947, and the tried-and-true two-banger put out 38.02 brake horsepower and 34.14hp at the drawbar with a gasoline engine and rubber tires, straining the dyno to 4,045lb of pull.

Augie's AO

Augie Scoto found his 1949 AO in a neighbor's shed, with ivy growing up through the crankcase. His neighbor used the machine in his operation, Fountain City Orchards, in the river bottom near Merced, California. The A was the first to offer a PTO as standard equipment, one of the major attractions for its first owner because his peaches needed lots of spraying and the PTO made that much easier than any alternative. "I restored this one because it is unusual," Augie says, "it is low to the ground and shrouded. It doesn't even have a three point hitch."

Augie's AO was built May 10, 1948 and shipped two days later. It went to a dealer in San Jose, California, at that time the center of the universe for plum, prune, and apricot growers. Well, the AO lived a long, productive life at Fountain City Orchards, and then it died. Augie dropped by his neighbor's place a few years ago to chat about irrigation allotments. He noticed a shrouded form in the shed, with just the radiator peeking out from under an old blanket and a mattress and a grimy JOHN DEERE visible in the gloom. "The ivy was growing up through the crankcase," Augie says. "It had lost oil pressure and the old owner pulled the cover to investigate, then he left it alone and abandoned it. The whole tractor was engulfed in ivy. And it was so low to the ground that I thought there wasn't much there. I paid him $200 for it and took it home on a lowboy."

John Deere Model B Tractor

The B came along in 1935, the A Model's smaller brother. The B was a little machine, designed for lighter work than the A, but it was just as successful; 300,000 sold over the course of production, the last going out the door in 1952. A lot of improvements to the little tractor were added over the years, with more power, styling, and gradually increasing weight. And the price, of course, grew with time; at the end of the line, in 1952, the B was listed at about $1,900, out the door.

Deere didn't claim a horsepower rating for the B when it first appeared. The specs

The cockpit of the BO is a little cramped and crowded. That's the 1gal gasoline tank visible at the top of the frame, used to get the B's engine going before switching over to the much cheaper kerosene in the large tank farther ahead.

At just 63in high and with a 41in tread, the BO can slither around in a crowded citrus grove with ease. If you stand on one brake at the end of a row, it will come around in just 8ft.

say, *Handles the load ordinarily pulled by four horses or mules.* Well, maybe not real big or muscular horses or mules, with the first engines. That caution was common at the time; nobody wanted to claim a performance level better than whatever the Nebraska tractor test measured (which had happened to several unfortunate manufacturers previously). The B, of course, used the same basic two-banger engine design but in a more petite version, and it has been rated independently as producing about 19hp (early engines) to 34hp (late gasoline model).

John Deere Model BO

The B was a boxy little creature for most of its life, and the BO, the orchard version of the model, never got the styling treatment the rest of the line received in 1947; the

BO was taken out of the lineup that year so all BO tractors are unstyled. Deere used a lot of cast steel in the machine, even if it was small; the BO weighed almost 3,000lbs without attachments and with the tanks dry.

But the orchard version was a short little tractor, only about 50in high, just the right size to fit under most fruit trees. That was about a foot shorter than the standard B (depending on when it was built and the variant) which usually stands about 63in high. It's tread was only about 41in, and the wheelbase was just 68in; this was a compact machine! Stand on one brake at the end of the row and you could turn the machine in just over 8ft—that was perfect for discing in the close quarters of many old orchards. With tracks instead of wheels, it was really low to the ground. Jack Cherry

says, "Lindeman also produced the crawler version—properly called the *Lindeman-John Deere BO.* Almost nobody ever refers to the tractor this way, but that's the way it is recorded in the archives and the way the tractor should be identified."

With nearly a third of a million Bs sold, the basic machine isn't exactly the most exotic or sought-after by collectors. The BO, though, is a different story, the most difficult "missing link" for somebody trying to put together a complete set of the B variants.

A total of 5,294 of the orchard version appear to have been sold. Doug Peltzer bought his BO in 1984, the first John Deere he bought as a collector. "It was a couple of years after that I realized I had the start on something special; that's when I got the idea to put together a set of John Deere orchard models."

Doug Peltzer doesn't have much trouble getting his BO started. Unlike most other tractors, the John Deere line used the flywheel on the left side for starting, an arrangement that worked a lot better once Deere made it a solid, smooth casting. Before that, folks tended to get caught in the spokes of the flywheel, breaking arms.

The John Deere Model 60 is essentially a Model A on steroids—the same solid foundation but with more power, live hydraulics, and a power-steering option after 1954. Inside that sleek green exterior beats the heart of a pumped-up Waterloo Boy 2-cylinder engine offering 40hp now.

John Deere Model 60 Orchard

The lettered models disappeared in 1952, replaced by the first of the numbered designs, the Model 50 and Model 60, then the Model 70 the following year, 1953. All had live hydraulics and power steering became an option in 1954. The 60 Orchard is really not much more than a Model A on steroids—bigger, stronger, but with the same solid, cast iron foundation, with essentially the same basic two-banger powerplant that went into the Waterloo Boy.

But this next-to-the-last generation of the A models was pumped up to about 42 brake horsepower, 37hp at the drawbar with the gasoline engine, a bit less with the all-fuel option. The engine was the same basic, slow-turning, high torque design of old, rated at 975rpm. The magneto ignition used on prior versions of the engine, though, was replaced by a 12-volt battery-based system. This new electrical and ignition system featured all the modern bells and whistles—a voltage regulator, starter, and even automatic spark advance; driving and warning lights were also standard on the Model 60.

It's a tight squeeze for Doug's John Deere Model unstyled A, but that's why the big citrus fenders were installed on tractors working this kind of grove. The unstyled A was the end of the long 2-cylinder line for Deere, a bulky engine by the time this machine was designed in the late 1950s. The unstyled A sold from 1956 to 1958 and was the only one of the "20s" to get the orchard treatment.

With six forward speeds and all that horsepower the Model 60 is a whiz at spraying and disking weeds, cutting furrows to control irrigation and pulling bin wagons and ladder racks during harvest. The addition of the duplex carb made the 60 run much better than previous Deere tractors and live hydraulics made the driver's job a lot easier.

Six forward speeds would propel you down the road at a blazing 11.25mph in top, or at a poky 1.5mph for deep plowing or spraying. A belt pulley was still standard equipment, rated at 3270fpm at 975rpm. PTO was standard, too, with a choice of two versions. One was a conventional transmission-driven type as standard equipment, the other an optional engine-driven "live" PTO with its own clutch that could be used independent of tractor ground speed.

The Model 60 was a bigger tractor all over: fuel capacity was up to 20gal for both engine options, with an extra gallon of gas for the all-fuel variant. The cooling system held 33qts. Rear tires were 14x26 size, on cast steel wheels, with 13x26 and 14x26 Low Pro-file tires available as an option. But all this bulk and power made for a tighter squeeze down the rows and around the last tree—overall width on the 60 was up to almost 76in (compared to 61in for the AO and 50in for the BO). Turning radius for the 60, though, was only 8in more than the old AO at 13ft 8in without differential braking. The 60 Orchard put on a few pounds with the years, too, at 5,332lb; the AO weighed only 4,088lb out the door.

Only 900 of the Model 60 Orchard variants appear on the Deere records, and Doug Peltzer bought the only one he's ever found, even though its engine had been destroyed by someone who ran it without oil.

Doug Peltzer on Deere Orchard Tractors over theYears

Probably the most noticeable thing about the 60 and the 620, compared to the earlier orchard tractors in the A family, was a result of the duplex carburetor. Tractors with the duplex carb just pulled the load smoother and ran better than before. They worked about the same in the orchard, in terms of rated power, but they started a load more easily and efficiently. And once the styled AO came in, there were real improvements in operator comfort. Power steering made a tremendous difference on the 620.

The most noticeable difference in orchard models from Deere in the 1930s and the 1950s or 1960s was the use of hydraulics. Once you had remote hydraulic controls, you didn't have to have the rope or crank to control your disc or plow. You didn't need a back-up technique to control the tool that was so important before. When Deere started offering hydraulics during the later production of the unstyled Model A orchard owners noticed a dramatic improvement in the kinds of tools you could use, and how you could use them! Before, you'd have to crank a disc up and down, or use a rope trip to control a furrowing machine. It was very hard to get into some of the corners where you needed to work.

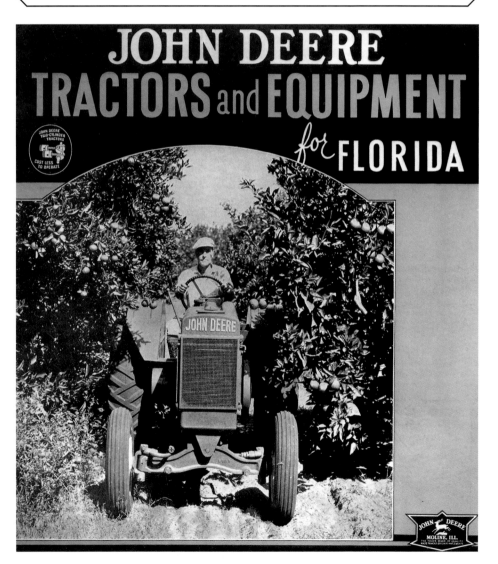

John Deere Model 620

The Model 620 was the end of a very long line of Deere Model A tractors. It had a design that originated with the GP so long ago, and an engine concept even older, with the Waterloo Boy.

Deere's so-called "-20" series had a short production life, from 1956 to 1958, based on evolutionary developments of earlier designs. The lineup included the 320, 420, 520, 620, 720, and 820 but only the 620 got the orchard treatment, and only 447 of those were built making them highly collectible. Even more exotic are the 620s with the LP fuel option, one of which Doug Peltzer owns. It came from a vineyard in the California central valley, and worked in a citrus grove in Tulare County.

The "-20" series was the end of the line for Deere's durable, legendary two-cylinder engine. While the design provided higher horsepower, all the iron required to keep a big bore, high-compression engine intact started to make for very bulky tractors. The driver of an 820 could hardly see the ground between the wheels because the big engine was blocking the view. The in-line four- and six-cylinder engines introduced in 1960 with the 1010, 2010, 4010, and 5010 models solved that problem pronto.

"The horsepower of today's orchard tractors remains just about the same as the output of those tractors back in the 1950s," Jack Cherry says. "Today's Deere machines are more nimble—you can drop the gear range and advance the throttle to get through the tough stuff today—the efficiency of today's tractors is excellent. But the early orchard tractors grew a heck of a lot of apples, oranges, and other fruit! If we still only had Model 60s and 620s to work with, orchard farmers would make out just fine."

J. I. Case

The J. I. Case company of today is nearly as old as John Deere and has just as illustrious a history in American commerce and agriculture. The company began in 1842 when young James Increase Case bought six primitive "ground hog" threshing machines in New York and carried them to the western fron-

LEFT
Brochure cover for John Deere citrus tractors and equipment, 1935.

tier—Wisconsin. He sold five of the six and used the last to custom-thresh small grain for farmers in Racine County. Case wore the little wooden machine out, then built a bigger and better machine, demonstrated it successfully over the next couple of seasons, and then went into the manufacturing business. The J. I. Case Company was born.

Unlike Deere, though, the J. I. Case Company specialized in harvesting machines rather than tillage tools at the beginning. Case became a giant "long line" company after the Civil War, producing steam tractors and threshing machines in abundance, and all sorts of plows, planters, and tillage tools, too. But Case steam engines and tractors, first offered in 1869, came to dominate the American farm market in the 1880s and 1890s. With this dominance of the farm tractive power market, it was natural that the company be interested in "infernal combustion" engines for their tractors when the technology began to mature around the turn of the last century.

Case actually built a gasoline-powered tractor in 1892—another version of the first gas tractor—but it didn't work very well and wasn't offered to the market. The real Case tractor program began design and develop-

Johnny Popper— Deere's Legendary Two-Cylinder Engine

Deere is a conservative company, in the best sense of the word, but the D and all subsequent models used a powerplant that was radically different from most tractors at the time. That engine was a massive, horizontal, slow-turning two-cylinder design with few moving parts and a distinctive exhaust sound that quickly earned an affectionate nickname for Deere's tractors, "Johnny Popper."

This same two-cylinder engine (with minor modifications) powered every Deere tractor from the 1920s to the 1950s, including the D, GP, A, B, 60, 620 orchard models shown in this book. The Deere two-cylinder engine would consume almost anything that was liquid and would burn—gasoline, kerosene, and inexpensive distillate. It was sturdy enough to be converted into a diesel, a modification Deere introduced during the 1950s. The design was so simple that farmers learned to do a lot of their own engine overhauls and major mechanical work. Access to the connecting rod bearing caps, for example, was designed to be extremely easy, encouraging the farmer to replace bearings as soon as they needed attention.

This powerplant, regardless of the tractor model, was designed to work best at about 1000rpm, about half the speed of four- and six-cylinder engines used in other tractors. The output, even at that slow speed, was enough power to work a pair of 14in plow bottoms behind even the little Model B.

Deere offered orchard variants of its basic models from the 1930s until the 620 grove model of the 1950s, the last in the catalog. However, you can still get a brand new Deere orchard tractor—but it will be a custom modified machine adapted by shops specializing in the conversion. Steve Van Dyer operates one of these in the central valley of California. He takes a stock 2355 and replaces the tires with low-profile rubber, adds big fenders to protect the limbs from the wheels, and lowers the seat and steering wheel. The result is a modern orchard tractor in green and yellow, maintaining the old tradition.

ment in 1910. The company built a prototype in 1911, and built a huge factory, the Tractor Works at Racine, Wisconsin, in 1913. Early models, like the 30-60, were still too big to do anything in the orchard except reduce the trees to stubble, but the little 12-25 of 1914 began to fit the bill.

The tiny Case 10-18 of 1918 certainly would fit in most orchards, and doubtless worked in some. This small machine was part of the long, legendary line-up of "cross-motor" Case tractors, offered in sizes suitable for just about any farm application. But the 10-18 and others of its time, although mechanically capable and small enough to fit between the rows, were covered with sharp angles that snag limbs and fruit in an orchard.

By 1937, when this rendering of the John Deere Model BO was made, Deere and the rest of the tractor industry were offering rubber tires as an alternative to the steel lugs of the standard wheel. *John Deere*

An early spring morning mist has left a damp sheen on the unstyled A. Rust is just one of the problems for old orchard tractors, although they're particularly vulnerable with all that sheet metal.

The shrouding on the unstyled A does a pretty good job of deflecting the foliage away from the driver. A trip down the rows will inevitably result in a sprinkling of blossoms. The delicious smell of a citrus grove in bloom is one of the great pleasures of this kind of farming.

RIGHT
J R Gyger's rotation plan for his Indiana farm is a simple one: *corn, soybeans, Florida*. The corn and soybeans keep him busy in the spring, summer and fall—it's off to Florida for the winter! And any farmer who spends much time in Florida will start noticing the exotic citrus tractors used in the groves down there. Gyger is a Case man, and pretty soon some of those Case orchards started making the northern migration with him in the spring. This Case Model DO is a beautifully restored example.

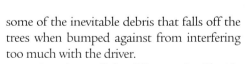

Over the next few years fruit growers whined and sniveled at their dealers, and the dealers passed the request on to the company: send us something designed for the groves! The first Case response was the CO.

Case Model CO

By 1934 Case was offering a variant of their popular Model C, the CO for orchard use. The CO featured big fenders to enclose the rear wheels (steel standard, rubber optional), and shrouds on the front wheels. The CO listed for about $1,000 on steel, $1,160 on rubber. Those tires were hefty 11.5x24in fronts, and 6x16 rear tires. This tractor relocated the air intake stack and added extensions to the fenders to keep some of the inevitable debris that falls off the trees when bumped against from interfering too much with the driver.

A variant of the CO was the Florida Special, a C on rubber, with full skirts, swinging drawbar, and without the differential brakes offered on the CO but not on the C. You could order wheel weights and an exten-

sion hub for the tractor, both at moderate additional cost. The Florida Special would set you back $1,083 sixty years ago, and apparently a lot of fruit growers thought it was worth it.

Case actually offered orchard fenders as an accessory item for both the Model L (which never appeared as a formal orchard variant)

and the standard Model C, allowing an owner to convert a conventional machine to grove use. Approximately 53,000 Case Model C tractors sold between 1929 and 1940, including just 1,280 of the orchard model.

The Model CO orchard tractor was built especially low and compact to allow operation among low-hanging limbs and fruit. Its full-

skirted, downward-sloping fenders lifted low-hanging branches and protected both tree and fruit from damage. The solid front wheel discs and smooth sides of the tractor left nothing to rake limbs when operated close to trees. The CO had the same engine and trans as were used on the CC. It also had differential turning brakes, which were great in tight turns and

The Case 730 is the 530's bigger brother, here towing a big sprayer around the grove. This one has the LP option, and plenty of sheet metal and guards to keep the citrus out of the works. *J. I. Case*

loose soils of a number of orchards. Production began in 1929 and lasted until 1938; 1,275 units were manufactured.

Rear tread width on the CO was fixed at 48ft. For work in the more narrow rows of vineyards, Case offered the Model CO Vineyard Special. Its wheel tread was reduced to 38in. The Vineyard Special was built in very limited numbers, beginning in 1935, and only 190 of these CO VS machines were man-

ufactured during the four year run that ended in 1939.

Case Model DO

It doesn't happen often in the tractor business, but the Case Model C was replaced in logical sequence by the D, in 1939. As usual, the basic machine was offered in a wide variety of variants, tricked out for specialized work as well as conventional applications. The lineup included the DV, a vineyard model with quite narrow track, the DO for orchard use, and the DOEX, an extremely rare export version of which only 115 were built.

All the Ds were part of Case's wonderful Flambeau Red series, a very modern (for the time, and still handsome today) design and a deep red-orange paint job that demands your full attention. Like most other tractors of the time, you could get the engine set up for one of a variety of fuels—gasoline, distillate, or LPG (heavily promoted by Case). The D stayed in production until 1953, although the DO was phased out the year before. During the long run over 104,000 Case Model Ds were built, including 2,874 of the DO version and 115 of the DOEX. By the end of the run, in 1952, the DO on rubber would set you back

Besides all the fender work, the DO had the exhaust turned down, out of the way, and the headlights repositioned low on the radiator casting to reduce snagging.

The operator's platform for the DO is a bit lower and a lot more protected than the standard D. Instrumentation is basic, air conditioning is not an option, but the steering wheel knob is an after-market option.

That color is "Flambeau Red," visible at five miles and a characteristic of the Case line during the 1950s when this gasoline DO was built.

$2,168. Gyger's was built in 1950 and is a standard gasoline model, one of many.

Case 400 Orchard Diesel (Case 402)

Although it says "400" on the hood, it is really a Case Model 402—the 400 is only a family name; the second digit, "0" identifies the tractor as a diesel, and the final "2" specifies an orchard variant. A 412 would be the same tractor with a gasoline engine.

The 400 series displaced the old and honorable Model D (in production since 1939), beginning in 1955. The Case version of Ford's three-point-hitch, the "Eagle hitch" was standard equipment—despite the objections of board chairman Leon Clausen, who thought it an unnecessary frivolity. But farmers were demanding hydraulics and the three-point-hitch, and Case finally surrendered with the 400. Clausen howled about this feature, and the dealers screamed back.

The standard versions got a foot clutch but the orchard model retained the hand control. Base price for the 400 was around $3,500, plus options, and the orchard model with diesel ran about $1,000 more. Hydraulics added a level of complexity and mechanical sophistication to what had been an essentially simple pulling machine and stationary power source, even with the PTO. Case designers put the pump just aft of the

Just one of over 104,000 Case Model D tractors, J R Gyger's is a nicely preserved example of the clan. It looks very much as it did new, back in 1950, when it sold for around $2,000.

No three-point hitch for this DO, and no hydraulic lift, either, but it was a successful, hard working machine anyway. Almost 3,000 of the model sold before the DO was dropped from the line in 1952.

clutch housing, with a quick-disconnect that let the operator disengage the system to save power and wear on the components.

The 400 introduced a lot of changes to the Case lineup. The Eagle hitch was one; it made changing implements a comparative snap—all done from the driver's seat, in just a few seconds, at least when all the pins were new and straight. For a lot of old farm boys, it was like they'd died and gone to heaven after years of struggling to hook up and connect old style implements. Another change, quite invisible, was the long-overdue replacement of the roller chain final drive—a good system in its time, but finally replaced by gears.

RIGHT
The Case 400-series orchard tractors came in your choice of LP, gasoline, or diesel fuel options; this one is a diesel. Base price for the 400 was around $3,500, diesel versions about $1,000 more. The 400s displaced the Ds in 1955.

Operator's station on the 400-series orchard models was well protected. Hydraulics were a new feature on Case tractors beginning with this model—over Board Chairman Leon Clausen's proverbial dead body. Clausen thought the system unnecessary and an expensive frivolity, objected loudly, but the market made him do it. The fittings are visible below the seat, left and right of the PTO.

Case wasn't shy about the way their tractors looked. Once they decided to style them, you could spot one a mile off, and the orchard models were the most stylish of all. Although they avoided the fins and chrome of the cars of the time, the influence of mid-1950s automotive design is strong in this glittering 400-series.

The 400 was available with gasoline, diesel, or LP engines. All used the same little four-banger block, with 4in bore and 5in stroke, displacing 251 cubes, generating about 45hp at the drawbar at 1,500rpm. Case made a big deal about the combustion chamber design, called the Powercel, claiming improved combustion. They repeated the theme with the basic engine, christened the Powerdyne. Typical of the time, the 400 used a 6 volt electrical system; a magneto was available as an option for the gas version and standard on the LP. The gas version was still available tricked out for distillate fuel, as an option. The orchard model came on rubber by this time, in size 13x26 on the rear. The diesel version weighed about 6,000lb, gas about 5,600lb.

"Mine was built in 1955," J.R. says, "and they only made 81 of them—that's one reason I like it so well. The DO is a nice tractor, too, but Case made them for years, by the thousands, and there are a lot of them around. The 400 series is special. I go to a lot of shows with my two-tone grove Case tractors, and I have

J R Gyger's 400 diesel is a 1955 product, one of only 80 manufactured with that engine. A 6-volt ignition system was still standard then, as were 13x26 rubber tires on the rear. The machine weighs about 6,000lb in the diesel version.

The snappy two-tone paint scheme of the 400-series is a bit of a show-stopper. The Gyger clan make restorations a family project. While most tractor restorations drag on for many months or years, the Gygers do a thorough, down-to-the-frame, makeover in just a couple of months.

The official designation for this tractor is the Case 414 but collectors and historians call it the "Pound Special." It is one of a batch of 120 built for the Pound Motor Company, a Case dealer whose Florida customers wanted—demanded—LP fuel for their tractors. This one was built in 1957.

RIGHT
Here's a family portrait of J R Gyger's Case orchard collection—a DO, a 400 LP "Pound Special," a 400 diesel, a 630 LP, and a 700 LP.

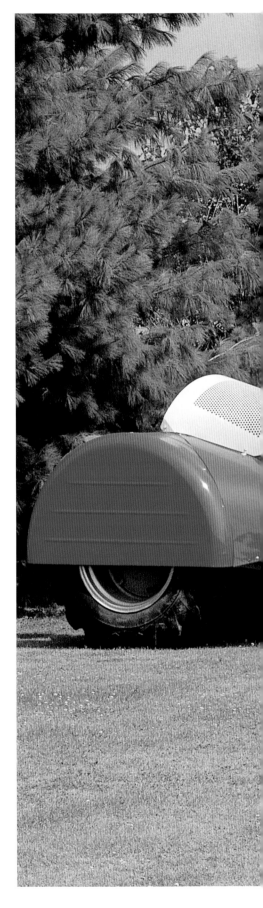

never seen another one. That adds to the fun of collecting them. And I like the appearance of the two-tone tractors, too."

Case 400 Orchard-LPG— "The Pound Special"

The official Case designation for this model is 414. J.R. Gyger's copy is a 1957 model, one of only 120 units built. "They called this one the "Pound Special" because a Florida Case dealer, the Pound Motor Company, wanted some tractors set up in a specific way. The factory built 120 of them to his specs, identified officially as the Model 414.

Case 630 Orchard (634)

The Case 600 series tractors arrived at the dealers in 1957, a bigger and beefier machine for America's orchards and fields. The 630 Orchard version is a small version of that large tractor, with a 188ci four-cylinder engine.

"My 630 is a 1961 product," Gyger says, "one of just fifty five of that model. Mine has the *Case-O-Matic* drive—but it's got a hand clutch! Figure that one out! They only offered that on a couple of models, making it especially rare.

Case 700 (715B)/730 Diesel

The Case 700 Series sold during just two years, 1958 and 1959—a virtually identical tractor to the 800 series sold at the same time, but with a dual-range, four speed transmission rather than the 800's torque converter drivetrain the company called Case-O-Matic.

The orchard model used the same basic powerplant installed in the row-crop, standard-tread, high-clearance, and tricycle versions, with the usual choice of three fuels—gasoline, LP, or diesel. This engine used the same 4in bore, 5in stroke Case engineers fell in love with years earlier. This engine, in the gasoline variant, displaced 251 cubes at a 6.5:1 compression ratio and put out about 54hp at 1,800rpm.

Owner Profile: J. R. Gyger

J. R. Gyger ("JR" to his friends) started farming in central Indiana, on rented ground, right after high school, back in the early 1960s. Over the years his operation grew and changed but one thing always stayed the same—his tractor was a Case, a new one just about every year. "My first tractor was a used SC," J. R. says, while I was in high school. I traded that one in on a brand

new 1962 Case DC. I traded that in on the 400—a fantastic tractor—then from the 400 to the 800, the 830, the 930, all the way up through the line. Over 37 years farming I owned 37 new Case tractors."

J. R. retired a few years ago but still likes Case tractors. Now he imports them, mostly from Florida, to his home place in Indiana where his son Jay still operates the farm. Orchard models are a specialty but not his exclusive interest, and J. R. sometimes picks up a Massey or International Harvester. The tractors go to shows now, not to the field, and the Gygers once took 13 tractors, all Case models, to one show.

The family pitches in on the restorations which typically take only a couple of intense months. One of the Gyger boys, Kyle, specializes in engine work. J. R. does the sheet metal, and Jay Gyger does the painting.

The process begins with a thorough cleaning with a pressure washer. All the wheels come off, all the fenders and sheet metal, and the basic tractor is supported on wooden blocks. Unlike most restorers, the Gygers don't sandblast the sheet metal or most of the castings because of the inevitable pitting of fenders and introduction of grit in bearings. Instead, they use a Makita orbital sander and rotary wire cut

This is the 630-series Orchard model, known officially as a 634 with this fuel option.

brush to clean off the old finish, rust, and dried fruit juice. "That takes the paint right down to the bare metal, and leaves everything real smooth," Gyger says, "unlike sandblasting that leaves everything with lots of little pits, or sanding discs that leave swirl marks on everything.

"After straightening and the prep work is done, we paint it—and we just use Case paint. It is good, glossy paint, but what I really appreciate about it is that you can get spray cans of the same color that match perfectly for touch-ups. You can't do that when you get your paint mixed up to a formula at an autofinishing supply shop."

LEFT
This example of the 630 was built in 1961 and has the *Case-o-Matic* drive but with the old-style hand clutch making it a very rare machine.

Rebuilding an orchard tractor, especially one with a lot of delicate sheet metal in the Florida climate, involves a lot of scrounging for parts and fabrication of missing shrouds and even fenders. "If I have only one side," Gyger says, "I'll lay it out and use it for a pattern to make the other. It's a lot of work!" The front tires typically need replacement, the rear tires usually are okay.

Massey-Harris
Massey-Harris Model 44

The 44 was one of the stylish post-war tractors that is so attractive to collectors today. The basic model was offered from 1947 until 1955 and was quite successful; nearly 100,000 were built in all configurations. Two engines were used, a Massey-designed H260 four and a Continental F226 six cylinder, both producing about the same amount of power. The K model was tested at Nebraska in late 1949. The four-cylinder I-head engine produced a

continued on page 69

LEFT
The Case 630 Orchard is part of a series that began production in 1957. While the standard models sold by the thousands, just 50 of these were built. This is how they looked back in the early 1960s, when they were new.

NEXT PAGE
The 630 uses a 188ci 4-cylinder engine rated at 2,000rpm with standard transmission, 2,250 with the torque converter *Case-O-Matic* option.

Continued from page 65

drawbar pull of 27.7hp in third gear at 4.29mph; a second test, in first gear, generated 4,629lb of pull at just under 2mph.

Dick Lamb's Massey-Harris Model 44 Orchard—A Very Rare Tractor

"I grew up on a farm in Indiana," Dick says, "it was just a small farm, but my uncle nearby had a large dairy farm we did a lot of custom hay bailing and combining, and I helped him. He always had Massey-Harris. That's where I fell in love with Massey-Harris." But Dick made a career with United Parcel Service as a supervisor, and recently retired. He has never been a farmer or a mechanic, but the love of the old red tractors was still alive. After he retired he pursued the interest by buying a few restored tractors, including a couple of Masseys and a John Deere or two. "But my ultimate desire was to own a 101 Super," Dick says. "I went to an auction where one was listed bound and determined to come home with it. It turned out to have been owned and restored by Dick Carroll who was well known for excellent restorations. I paid more than twice what I had intended—but I came home with a 101 Super!"

You won't see this Case 630 rubbing shoulders with citrus trees after all the work the Gyger family invested in that sheet metal and paint. With the *Case-O-Matic* transmission, the 630 had 12 forward speeds from 1.6mph to 21.6mph.

LEFT
Tractors don't usually get such loving treatment during their working lives but a select few fall into the hands of people who respect and admire these handsome machines. This is a Case 700 series orchard model, produced during 1958 and 1959, in showroom fresh condition.

The 700 was sold with LP, diesel, or gasoline engine options. All used the same basic engine block found in the standard models, a 4in bore, 5in stroke four-cylinder design putting out about 54hp at 1,800rpm.

Dick picked up a set of tractor cards featuring the 101 Super, and in the set was a card for another Massey-Harris model, the 44 Orchard. "My wife saw that and just *ooohed* and *ahhed* over the 44 Orchard. She said, 'I'd really like to have one of those some day.' So I started looking at the ads but never saw one advertised. Seeing that card was the first time I even knew orchard models of the Massey even existed!"

Dick took his lovely 101 Super to a show at Perry, Iowa. After unloading the tractor Dick looked around and, just down the row, there was a sparkling 44 Orchard model! The 44 belonged to Dick Carroll, a well-respected Massey-Harris collector and restorer, home-based in Alta Vista, Kansas.

Carroll had done the restoration job on the 101 Super, so the two conspired about the paternity of that machine. During the conversation, Lamb steered the conversation over to the orchard model. "I mentioned how beautiful the orchard tractor was," he recalls, "and told Dick Carroll that the 44 Orchard was a tractor my wife wanted to own someday. I asked him if he knew of any—in any condition at all—that might be for sale or coming up at auction."

Carroll said that he only knew of seven or eight in existence and none of those for sale. Then he had an idea. "I just oughta sell ya that one!" Carroll said. "I couldn't believe it," Dick Lamb says. But Carroll was serious; he was ready to cut back on the collection

and he wanted to think it over, discuss the possibility with Mrs. Carroll, and have a decision the next day.

The Lambs talked it over, too, and came up with a price they could afford for the rare 44 O.

The next day the tractor was indeed for sale, but the asking price and offer were about $2,500 apart. After a bit more negotiation, the deal was made and Mrs. Lamb became one of the few, the proud, the owners of Massey-Harris 44 Orchard tractors. "The next day my wife came to look at her new tractor. She was thrilled! She had no regrets then or now! We've taken it to shows and just had a ball sharing it with other people and talking about Massey-Harris."

Betty and Dick Lamb don't have many apple trees on their place in Milo, Iowa, but they do have one of the prettiest and most exotic orchard tractors in the country, a Massey-Harris Model 44 Orchard. Only a handful of these exist anywhere, only one other in restored condition. And this one really belongs to Betty who saw a picture of one and admired it. Dick bought it for her not long after, one of only two restored 44 Orchards anywhere. Betty wins "Best of Show" award in the Tractor Collector Wife division.

It has been a popular exhibit, and naturally other collectors drool at the thought of acquiring the 44 Orchard. The Lambs have been offered $20,000 for it—much more than they paid, not nearly enough to pry it out of their grasp. That says something about the wisdom of the investment, though. Conventional restored tractors sell for around $4,000, so one is lucky to get the direct expenses back from a restoration project.

Besides the Lamb 44 O, and another restored machine in Michigan (the one on the card), Massey-Harris collectors can only identify half a dozen or so orchard models still in existence, in any condition. There are two in Arizona, neither restored, and one in Nebraska. The only known restored examples are the Michigan tractor and the one owned by the Lambs. According to the factory serial number list, fewer than 200 were ever manufactured, so this scarcity isn't surprising. But it makes the Massey-Harris 44 Orchard tractor a very rare and beautiful beast indeed.

Oliver
Hart-Parr and Oliver

It doesn't seem fair that one tractor company gets to revolutionize the agricultural equipment company twice in its lifetime. Other tractor builders, dozens of them, faded from existence, barely leaving a trademark in the sands of agricultural history. But Hart-Parr Company of Charles City, Iowa introduced the first gasoline-powered traction engine and then popularized the name "tractor" for their machine. Founded in 1901, the Hart-Parr Company gets the credit for starting the tractor industry.

Then, thirty-five years later, in the middle of the Great Depression, they took another quantum leap forward. They introduced a tractor so radically new that the industry scrambled for several years to copy and catch up. Reorganized as the Hart-Parr Oliver Company in 1928, the new management developed

The Massey-Harris 44 was a stylish, successful post World War II design that sold in all variants about 100,000 copies, with under 200 orchard models included. Production lasted from 1947 until 1955. This one was restored by Dick Carroll, a Massey-Harris collector and restoration specialist from Alta Vista, Kansas.

the first "styled" tractor, the 70, in 1935.

The Oliver 70 featured an aerodynamic design with a 6-cylinder engine and an electric starter. It took its name from the 70 octane fuel that provided its power; it ran on the same gasoline that was now widely available for motor cars. Once again the industry was stunned. It took several years before the competition recovered enough to hustle a similar product to the showroom. But the Oliver 70 had already conquered the marketplace and the title as "the prettiest tractor ever built."

The Hart Parr Company was first formed by two University of Wisconsin students, Charles Hart and Charles Parr, in Madison, Wisconsin in 1897. The company was later acquired by the venerable Oliver Chilled Plow Works in 1928. It was a time of corporate mergers in the agricultural equipment industry, with many implement and plow manufacturers forming partnerships with tractor builders. Reorganized just before the Depression, the

The 44 came with a choice of two engines, a 4-cylinder designed and built by Massey-Harris or a 6-cylinder F226 from Continental. The 4-cylinder produced about 4,600lb of drawbar pull in first gear at 2mph.

LEFT
That's a tight squeeze when you climb aboard the Massey-Harris 44 O—there isn't a lot of room for your feet. But the seat and platform are low and well shrouded from the dangers of passing limbs.

This is a revolution on wheels, the Oliver Model 70 in orchard dress. The 70 transformed the tractor industry starting in 1935. The 70 was first with a 6-cylinder engine, and the "70" is a reference to the 70-octane fuel that fed it. This tractor was the first to incorporate the sleek, aerodynamic lines that came to be called the "styled" look in tractors. It is often called "the prettiest tractor ever built," and the orchard version is the prettiest of the 70s.

RIGHT

Everett Jensen grew up on an Oliver 70, but not an orchard model. Then he went to work for an Oliver dealer for a couple of years, infecting him with a lifetime case of the Oliver bug. There is no known cure for this condition except a full set of green tractors with yellow trim—which don't have two cylinder engines. This one came from Texas with a stuck engine and a lot of black goo in the transmission. The sheet metal was in the right spots but badly dented.

The Oliver 70 Orchard model, along with the other variants, went through some changes over the years. This early photograph, intended to be used in heavily rendered illustrations for advertisements, shows a first-generation version of the 70, built until 1938. *Oliver - Hart-Parr Archives, Floyd County Museum, Charles City, Iowa*

new company lost no time in producing a new rowcrop tractor and a full line of implements. But their finest creation was the Oliver 70, the tractor that first came out in 1935.

The Oliver Company has disappeared. Merged, bought out and reorganized, the Hart-Parr Oliver plant in Charles City wore the corporate logos of several other corpora-tions in the last decades; the last name on the plant was the New Idea Company. The plant itself was demolished in 1994.

70 Orchard

The Oliver 70, introduced first in 1935, is a milestone machine. It turned the tractor industry on its ear and provoked a series of changes that are still visible today, in modern tractor design. Prior to the 70, tractors were clunky, visually complicated, strictly utilitarian machines. They all had a crank up front for a starter, most had a simple two- or four-cylinder engine, and were plain. The 70 was the first to adopt a trend then starting in the automobile industry—smoother curves and contours, an

Another view of the early generation Oliver 70 Orchard but with steel wheels instead of rubber. The 70's 6-cylinder engine, with its smooth running and ample power, along with the sleek lines and numerous features, made the 70 a milestone product in the tractor industry. *Oliver - Hart-Parr Archives, Floyd County Museum, Charles City, Iowa*

integrated shape, a look that quickly acquired a name: *"styled."* It was extremely handsome in 1935, and when it was redesigned in 1937 the 70 became even more beautiful externally and quite innovative mechanically.

The Oliver 70 not only had a radical appearance, it was radical under the sheet metal, too. It was the first to offer a 6-cylin-

der engine, an electric starter, a six-speed transmission, and lights as standard equipment. The competition sneered at first—then scrambled to catch up. Deere followed suit beginning in 1938 but their machines looked coarse and clunky for a generation afterwards. In fact, few tractors have come close to the lovely effect of the Oliver 70 in any ver-

sion, and even fewer compete with the Orchard model.

The Oliver 70 applied automotive styling concepts to the tractor: rounded, "aerodynamic" lines, at a time when most tractors were angular, boxy machines with sharp corners and a "bolted together" appearance.

That electrical tape on the steering wheel is an after-market detailing touch, an authentic—if not original—addition to a lot of tractors of this vintage.

Oliver 70, right side detail.

LEFT
This 70 rolled off the assembly line in 1945, over half a century ago, but the rear tires are apparently original and much of the tractor is pretty much stock. Oliver built 897 of the 70 that year but how many were orchard variants isn't recorded.

Plowing a citrus orchard with an Oliver Model 70 Orchard. Citrus groves are very long-lived and have a tendency to grow together to form hedges. In fact, without pruning, a citrus grove would form a solid mass of vegetation within a few years. That creates special problems for the grower and the tractor operator working out in the trees. *Oliver - Hart-Parr Archives, Floyd County Museum, Charles City, Iowa*

The 70 was introduced as a row crop tractor first, at serial number 200001 in 1935, and the 70 Standard a year later at 300001. It is unclear just when the orchard modifications were offered (the serial number lists don't indicate orchard models) but apparently the 70 Row Crop was available as an orchard variant from the very beginning in 1935. This habit of including an orchard variant along with the standard or row crop models was an old one with Oliver; the earlier 18-28 model from the early 1930s was like-wise offered as row crop, rice field, industrial, and orchard versions.

Owner Profile: Everett Jensen

"I grew up on an Oliver 70," Everett Jensen says, "and after high school I worked as a mechanic for an Oliver dealer for a couple of years. Then as time went on, after thirty years, I got to thinking about that old Oliver 70 tractor that I used to drive. So I bought one just like my father used to own. Well, one led to a second, and then there were

four . . . and that's how I got to be an Oliver collector."

Everett started putting together a set of Oliver 70s—a Row Crop, a Row Crop with the single front wheel, a wide front model, a standard tread, an industrial model—but no orchard model, the final variant on the breed. Then one appeared in the Minneapolis classi-

Oliver brochure cover, circa 1948. *Oliver - Hart-Parr Archives, Floyd County Museum, Charles City, Iowa*

"The "70" ORCHARD AND GROVE

OLIVER

Disking a citrus orchard, sometime in the mid-1930s. *Oliver-Hart-Parr Archives, Floyd County Museum, Charles City, Iowa*

fied ads, offered by what some folks in the tractor collecting field call "relocators." They are also known as antique tractor "jockeys," dealers who make a business of buying and selling antique collectable tractors and who often move machines from one part of the country to another in search of better prices.

"I called the guy. He had found the tractor in Texas and brought it to Minnesota to sell. I bought it over the phone, sight unseen. The guy delivered it, and the tractor was just as advertised—four flat tires, the engine was stuck tight, but all the parts were

there. The dealer didn't know the work history of the machine but we both surmised that it hadn't been used in an orchard much. Since the 70 Orchard and the 70 Standard were almost identical except for the tin work, we figured it got used for standard field work and maybe row crops. But we got the engine loose, and it cleaned up pretty well!"

There wasn't a lot of mechanical work to be done, once the engine was unstuck and the goo cleaned out of the crankcase and transmission. There was quite a bit of body work required, though, and that was done by

David Swanson. The front tires needed replacement but the rear ones were okay. "Other than that, it's quite original." Everett's 70 Orchard is a 1945 model, SN 310276. Oliver built, according to the records, 897 of the 70 that year, but how many were orchard models isn't known, according to Jensen.

McCormick-Deering– International Harvester

We call it the Farmall. It's a terrific name for an agricultural machine, a name

Factory photograph, Model 77. *Oliver - Hart-Parr Archives, Floyd County Museum, Charles City, Iowa*

that says it all. The Farmall is the machine for all farms. Designed, developed and delivered by an extremely profitable and powerful agricultural equipment builder, the Farmall is nevertheless a machine that delivers on its considerable promises.

The Farmall is the direct descendent of the man who mechanized farming, visionary and inventor Cyrus McCormick and the company that came to be called McCormick-Deering. Considered the father of American agriculture, Cyrus McCormick built and demonstrated the first successful reaping machine in 1831. His machine marked the true beginnings of mechanized farming, a historic event in American economic development as well as the chronicle of farming across recorded history. But he neglected to file for a patent on the machine until 1834; his attention was focused on the development of the McCormick cast-iron plow. Too late, a Mr. Obed Hussey had secured a patent for his own machine a year earlier. The two men would compete in public demonstrations and in the courtroom for the next seventeen years.

When this legendary company is referred to today, enthusiasts are likely to say McCormick, or the initials "I. H." or some-times you still hear an old-timer call it "Deering." That's the nickname for the eight companies that merged to make up the International Harvester Company nearly a century ago.

Negotiations for a merger were started in 1890 but not completed until 1902. When the chaff had settled and the ink was dry, the International Harvester Company had been formed by the eight companies who signed the agreement; the McCormick Harvesting Machine Company, the Deering Harvesting Machine Company, the Plano Manufacturing Company, Warder Bushnell & Glessner, the Milwaukee Harvesting Company, D.M

Plowing under the cover crop. Several forms of orchard cultivation have been popular over the years. At the beginning of the 20th century many farmers used the orchard as a kind of pasture, grazing livestock among the trees. This was particularly favored for poultry in summer when shade could keep a flock healthy and productive. Many farmers also planted cover crops between the trees, then disked them under later; this provided organic material and helped with water absorption. *Oliver - Hart-Parr Archives, Floyd County Museum, Charles City, Iowa*

Osborne & Company, Aultman Miller Company and the Minneapolis Harvester Company. McCormick and Deering, the two largest companies of the new group, finally merged to form McCormick-Deering, after ten years of negotiations.

International Harvester developed the power-take off (PTO), that extraordinarily useful refinement that allowed the tractor to operate a binder as it was being pulled. Staff engineer Ed Johnston had seen the device in France where an inventive farmer had modified a McCormick binder, powering the machine with an extension shaft sticking out the back of the tractor. Power take-off devices quickly became standard on Farmall machines

The improved "Farmall" with all the bells and whistles made its formal debut in 1923. The name was trade-marked and the advertising campaign informed the farmers that "If it isn't a McCormick-Deering, it isn't a Farmall" and the tag line said "Made only by International Harvester." It was the first response to Ford's challenge for supremacy in the marketplace.

Oliver 70 Orchard brochure, circa 1948. *Oliver - Hart-Parr Archives, Floyd County Museum, Charles City, Iowa*

The Oliver Orchard and Grove "70"

THE OLIVER ORCHARD AND GROVE "70"

For two years the Oliver "70" has been showing the world how good a tractor can be. Thousands of operators have been glad they had the good judgment to buy it as their *first* tractor—thousands of others have bought a "70" when they learned what they really wanted in a tractor. It has established a high place for itself by what it does and how it does it.

Now, that famous performance and endurance have been given the beauty of a fine thoroughbred. Today, when you buy your Oliver Orchard and Grove "70", you get the neatest, nimblest tractor with the sweetest performing power plant that ever worked close to tree trunks or lugged a heavy sprayer.

The Oliver Orchard and Grove "70" literally has everything you want in a tractor for your orchard or grove, smooth, unfaltering power from six, husky cylinders—self-starter—performance that all tractor manu-

facturers know is ONLY possible with an engine designed especially for the fuel it uses.

Is it low? Lower than ever before. The steering wheel is lowered and you operate it from the new low upholstered sponge rubber-cushioned seat or from the platform at drawbar height. Steering is as quick and easy as your automobile.

Is it streamlined? More than any tractor in tractor history—radiators, wheels, fenders, exhaust carried down under the hood—nothing, absolutely nothing projecting to catch branches or injure trees.

The "70" dodges around your trees as nimbly as a polo pony—drives as easily as the family car, rides like a hammock on the road or working among your trees.

Your Oliver Orchard "70" does every orchard or grove job and does it well.

2

IT'S JUST GOOD JUDGMENT TO GET AN OLIVER "70"

THE OLIVER "70"—IT'S THE "6"

Spraying citrus with an Oliver Model 70 Orchard tractor, circa 1935. *Oliver - Hart-Parr Archives, Floyd County Museum, Charles City, Iowa*

This McCormick-Deering 10-20 has been in Doug Peltzer's family since it was new in 1924 and it has always worked in the citrus groves of the far west.

McCormick-Deering, later formed the foundation for International Harvester, shared the tractor industry limelight with many competitors during the 1930s, and—like the competition—offered orchard and grove variants to its basic field tractors. For McCormick-Deering that was the O-12 in the early 1930s, then the 0-14 late in the decade.

McCormick-Deering Orchard and Grove Tractor Model O-14 (1939)

The O-14 was a low, short, machine, a smaller version of the company's then-standard farm tractor, the W-30. It was only four feet high, with a 15hp four-cylinder engine and a tiny 60in wheelbase. Stomp on the gas (or kerosene, if you preferred) and the little machine would rocket up to redline, a blistering 2000rpm that would propel you up to the upper performance limit, about 10.5mph. Rack the wheel hard over at the end of the row and your little O-12 would almost pick its own pocket, turning in just 9ft 3in. Rubber tires were standard on this machine, as was a PTO. The seat adjusted forward and aft, up and down. Optional equipment included electric lights, starter, belt pulley (attached to the PTO), and padded seat.

McCormick-Deering Orchard and Grove Tractor Model 10-20 (1939)

McCormick-Deering offered a larger version of the O-12, the 10-20. This tractor, again based on the W-30 but not quite as powerful, was designed to plow seven to twelve acres a day (the W-30 would do nine to thirteen, according to the factory). This ver-

The McCormick-Deering 10-20 Orchard was promoted as capable of plowing 7 to 9 acres a day, a pretty beefy machine for its time. That specification changed over the production life of the design, up to 12 acres in 1934 literature.

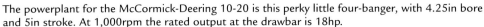
The powerplant for the McCormick-Deering 10-20 is this perky little four-banger, with 4.25in bore and 5in stroke. At 1,000rpm the rated output at the drawbar is 18hp.

sion came on steel as standard equipment, with rubber optional. The engine's 4.25in x 5in cylinders operated at 1000rpm max, yielding 18hp at the drawbar. It was considerably bigger in every respect, including turning radius—13ft.

McCormick-Deering 10-20

Doug Peltzer's 10-20 has been in the family since it was new, back in the 1920s. It originally belonged to his grandfather who used it on a citrus grove near Anaheim, California, on ground that is now Disneyland. "My collection started with the family 10-20 McCormick-Deering. I remember riding on that tractor as a kid of seven or ten years old with my dad as he disced weeds and furrowing out our orange groves in the Anaheim area. The tractor was bought new in 1926 by my grandfather. I remember my dad taking that tractor from grove to grove in the area—four of them within a ten mile radius—with all the implements trailing behind on rubber or steel road wheels. He tossed his bicycle on someplace and waddled off down the county road."

Owner Profile: Dan Schmidt

"I got my O-12 in 1987, from Benton Harbor, Michigan," Dan reports, "right out of the apple orchard! It had been setting for

a number of years, though, and was in pretty sad shape. It took almost two years to repair the fenders alone—they were really rusty and pitted. The whole project took about three years. The radiator had a big hole in it, the tires were shot, too, but at least the engine wasn't stuck. We put new tires on it, a new clutch, new brakes, completely overhauled the engine, new wheel bearing on one front wheel. That little tractor has 27 roller- or ball-

The foundation for the McCormick-Deering 10-20 Orchard was an extremely successful and popular field tractor, the standard 10-20; the orchard version didn't yet have the extensive shrouds and fenders but it did get a lower seat, lower wheels front and rear, "aprons" for the drive wheels, a lower steering wheel, and high skid rings for the front wheels.

LEFT
That's the spark advance control for the McCormick-Deering's 4-cylinder engine, a relic of the days before such things were automated.

The 10-20's engine is a simple system, energized by this International magneto. Like almost everything on this tractor, it is an original—over sixty years old and still going strong.

After-market steel wheels were a common installation on orchard tractors in citrus groves. These came from the Kay Brunner foundry in Los Angeles. The extra weight and smooth surface were helpful in the groves.

bearings in it! Mine was built in 1937. I only know of five or six others."

McCormick-Deering OS-4 (Orchard Special)

Just before and then after World War II, International Harvester's McCormick-Deering division began offering quite beautiful styled tractors to compete with those from Deere, Case, and the rest of the industry. The foundation of this line was the standard W-4 series, available in modified form for orchard use as the OS-4 Orchard Special.

This model sold from 1940 to 1953. Over 34,000 of the basic W-4 design sold but

Ira Matheney found this W-30 Orchard in a shed where it had been parked for 25 years. Believe it or not, that is the original paint there under the rust and grime.

very, very few orchard models were made during those fourteen years; the records don't provide specific numbers but there are almost none around. K. R. Withrow has one, though, and it's a beauty.

His 1948 example has a 4-cylinder engine identical to the powerplant used in the Farmall Model H, with 3.75in bore and 4.25in stroke. The Nebraska test rated this engine in the W-4 at 21.12hp drawbar and 24.3hp on the pulley; fuel consumption was a piddling 2.05 gallons per hour under full load. The tractor weighs 3,816lb.

Despite its long sleep, Ira's W-30 fired right up once the mouse nests were cleaned out of the carb and some fresh gas sloshed into the tank. It runs—not like a watch, exactly, but a performance of any kind under the circumstances is a testament to the construction of this senior citizen of the tractor community.

The McCormick-Deering OS-4 differs from the standard W-4 in ways typical of all orchard models of the era:
- Over-center hand clutch—required because of the low seat position;
- Dropped brake pedals, for the same reason;
- Narrow width rear wheel base;
- Dropped platform, seat, and steering wheel;
- Solid rim front wheels to keep from snagging limbs and fruit;
- Air intake re-plumbed to below hood, to avoid snags;
- Exhaust rerouted to lower left side of engine;
- Super low "granny" gear (half the speed of first gear on the W-4) for spraying operations;
- Lights repositioned to below the front cowl to avoid snags.

Withrow's OS-4 was a sorry sight when he found it at an antique tractor dealers' lot. The previous owner had worked on the engine—and put it back together without connecting rod

bearings! It was rough and rusty and rare—a difficult combination to pass up when you like the look of those old McCormick-Deering models.

"I believe it'll run," the dealer said, as they fired it up for the first time.

"I believe I will shut it off!" K. R. said when he heard the engine slamming itself to death.

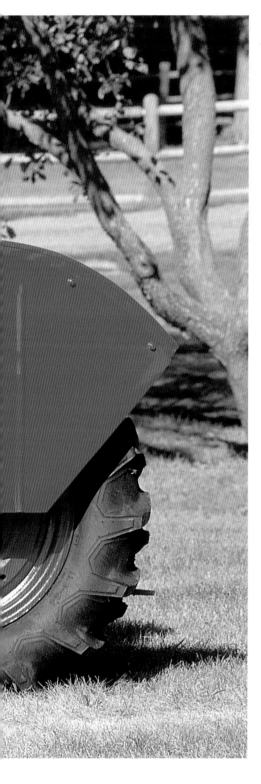

The McCormick-Deering O-12's radiator cap is this handsome casting. It is missing from many other examples—ejected into orbit after an overheat, perhaps, or snitched by somebody who just liked its shape.

LEFT
Now here is what they looked like sixty years ago: a pristine 1937 McCormick-Deering 0-12, the baby of the orchard family from International Harvester. Dan Schmidt bought his right out of the apple orchard near Benton Harbor, Michigan, where it once worked for a living—but it didn't look like this then.

The spark advance lever for the O-12 is mounted high on the steering column, easier to reach than the one on the 10-20 owned by Doug Peltzer.

But the serial number on the block proved it was the original so the machine was purchased and carried home to Sherman, Texas.

It needed a new crankshaft, new sleeves and pistons—among other things. But it was ready to show in June of 1995. "It looks pretty good now," Withrow reports, "and it has all its original equipment in the right places—even connecting rod bearings. The drop seat position is low, and the rear treat is a lot narrower than the standard tractor. You can barely see over the hood, and the foot brakes are positioned low on each side. Because of the need for spraying, the rear end

You wouldn't know it now, but Dan's O-12 had a big hole in the radiator when he bought it in 1987. It runs perfectly now and is a standout at the farm shows in the area around Omaha, Nebraska, where Dan lives.

is geared to just half the speed of the standard model. I've never seen another one—and I like to see unique tractors at a show. It seems to be unique."

Orchard Tractors Today

The quaint, curious, oddball tractors collectors will be looking for in the year 2040 are coming off the assembly line today. Case, New Holland, and Deere all offer versions designed just for the fruit industry. Just as in the past, these are variants of small standard tractors adapted to grove use.

Deere seems to have the most extensive lineup today, just as in the past. Deere's current models are part of the 5000 and 6000 series.

The tractor had been sitting in an apple orchard for several years, uncovered, and the sheet metal was in poor condition. It took two years to fix the fenders, three years to complete the project. The engine wasn't stuck, at least, and most of the parts were present. The tires, clutch, brakes, and one wheel bearing have been replaced; the engine was thoroughly overhauled. Only five or six such O-12s are known to exist.

The 5000 series use engines rated at between 40 and 73hp; the 5200, 5300, and 5400 all use three-cylinder powerplants displacing 2.9 liters. The turbocharged 5500 displaces 3.9 liters from four cylinders, yielding 73hp. All come with rear-wheel drive as standard, mechanical front wheel drive as an option.

The orchard versions of the 6000 line came out in 1994, starting with the 6500L (the L is for *Low Profile*). These tractors are in the 65 to 85hp range. These tractors are bigger than their grand-daddies. The 6500L is 163in long, with a 94.5in wheelbase and a turning radius of about 14.7ft without differential braking. The overall width varies, depending on tires, from about 84in to 100.6in, and vertical clearance is as little as 61in. Citrus fenders aren't offered on these Deere tractors, but you can still get them from aftermarket manufacturers.

Deere's Jim Beebe says, "A lot of growers today are planting their trees closer together and keeping the growth closer to the ground, for a variety of reasons. They want tractors that are more compact, and that's what we are trying to give them. We don't offer the full fenders, but we do offer low profile tires that reduce the height of the machine considerably. Our standard tractor has a 34in rim and we're offering orchard models with 16.5in rims—that gets the tractor very low. We are also offering high clearance drawbars, for those that want them, and a high clearance fuel tank. Our low profile tractors have a reversable steering wheel that can give you an additional 2in of clearance. The 6500L was developed for the California market where extra power was needed for the big air sprayers commonly used out there."

Here's what an McCormick-Deering OS-4 looks like new, or nicely restored. This example belongs to K R Withrow and was a very sorry sight when discovered at an antique tractor dealer's lot a few years ago. It had been worked on by a previous owner who assembled the engine without bothering to include connecting rod bearing caps. K R discovered the problem when the dealer fired it up to demonstrate how well it ran. *K R Withrow*

K R Withrows' OS-4 lacks the big citrus fenders but is otherwise a complete and proper McCormick-Deering orchard model: over-center clutch, low seat, narrow wheel track, solid front rims, re-plumbed intake and exhaust, and a super low "granny" first gear are just some of the modifications to the basic W-4 foundation. *K R Withrow*

NEXT PAGE
John Deere Model 6200L. This tractor uses a 4-cylinder turbocharged diesel engine to generate 66hp at the PTO at 2,300rpm. Twelve forward speeds, plus even lower "creeper" speeds, make the tractor adaptable to most orchard chores. *John Deere*

This John Deere Model 5400N is one example of the modern breed of orchard tractors. The mandatory roll-over-protection (ROP) makes it a tall tractor, but it folds down if required. *John Deere*

John Deere Model 5400N mowing the orchard floor. The 5400 models use 3-cylinder engines and yield 60 PTO horsepower at 2,400rpm. *John Deere*

NEXT PAGE
John Deere Model 6500L (with after-market wheel covers) applying "bloom" spray. This is a 95hp tractor with Deere's *PowerQuad* torque-converter transmission; twelve speeds forward and reverse are standard, 16 optional. *John Deere*

CHAPTER 3

CRAWLER TRACTORS

As mentioned before, crawlers have some major virtues that make them popular in the vineyards and orchards, particularly in the rolling hills of the west. You won't see many working in Iowa or the apple orchards of Michigan, but you won't see many wheeled tractors in the citrus groves of Riverside County, California, either.

Crawler tractors are rough-riding, slow, and a nuisance to trailer from orchard to orchard. One gets more done in a day on a wheeled tractor. It is cheaper and easier to use—within its limits. In many western operations, there are times when the crawler is the only option. In the spring, when farmers like Doug Peltzer disc, the heavy soil on the hillsides produces big clods the size of your fist. It's the kind of condition that makes wheeled tractors sit on ground, tires spinning! Doug says, "A crawler will just walk through ground like that. The wheeled tractor is a *farming* tractor, but even so there are times when we go get our old 1949 Cat D2 because it is the ideal machine for what we need to do."

The work Doug needs to do is often deep chisel plowing, or discing on a slope when the grass is as slippery as grease. A crawler will do both jobs when a wheeled tractor can't. And a crawler is much more gentle to the ground, with a lighter ground pressure that keeps

Crawlers are, despite all that cast-iron bulk, gentle on the ground. That's because the weight is distributed over a much greater area. The result is better traction, less soil compaction (a major problem in groves) and greater stability on slopes.

"plow sole" or "hard pan" from forming.

So back before World War II and for a few years after, the vast acreages of western fruit trees from the Mexican border all the way to Canada were worked mostly with Holts, Bests, Caterpillars, Cletracs, Oliver crawlers, International Harvestor tracklayers, Allis-Chalmers and Lindeman-John Deere tracked machines. And many of them are still around—they were made of good steel and it takes a long time for all that iron to rust away or wear out. Some are parked in the corner of a grove, where they died, and others are lined up nice and neat in private collections. But the companies who built them aren't as familiar to most tractor fans as Deere, Minneapolis-Moline, Case, and the rest of the giants. So here's a little background on another side of the orchard tractor business.

Cletrac-the Cleveland Tractor Company

Organized in 1916, the Cleveland Tractor Company was an early builder of crawler tractors. The White brothers, Clarence and Rollin, came from a family that had already experienced considerable financial success with White motor vehicles and White sewing machines. Visiting San Francisco during the 1915 Panama-Pacific Exposition, they had seen the agricultural machinery displayed by the Best Company. Best was showing four tractors as well as a harvester, plows, a land leveler and a sagebrush clearing machine. The White's quickly bought a Best prototype.
continued on page 106

Cletrac "crawler" tractors have been a part of Bill Bechtold Jr.'s family for about fifty years, and part of the orchard business for a lot longer than that. Bill Jr. is disking under the winter's weeds as the young peaches in this grove bloom like crazy. This Cletrac Model AD is part of the Bechtold family fleet of about 65 crawlers, all Olivers or Cletracs. You'd think they have pretty well cornered the market on Cletracs but another collector, Arthur Bright, has a working fleet of about the same size nearby.

Caterpillar has long dominated the crawler tractor market, and here's an example of a very popular model for the fruit growing industry of the 1930s. It is a Caterpillar Model 22, built in 1935 and doing the same job it has always done, disking an orange grove near Irvine, California. It belongs to Richard Walker whose family has been in the citrus industry for several generations. *Richard Walker*

continued from page 103

Best crawlers were nearly identical to Holt crawler-tractors; the two California companies were rivals. The Holt company had recently completed a major project with their tracked machines, construction of the mammoth Los Angeles aquaduct in South-

ern California. Crawler tractors were already essential to profitable farming operations in the San Joaquin delta where sandy soils swallowed conventional sreel-wheeled tractors. Now crawlers were proving valuable for all sorts of construction and industrial jobs. Rollin White saw the possibilities.

But Rollin White had also watched a Yuba Ball Tread Tracklayer operating in the field and was impressed with its performance. The Yuba Ball Tread machines had also been developed in the California delta country to cope with the marshy soil. Convinced that there was a market for small,

106

inexpensive crawlers, White acquired the prototype Best crawler with the intention of putting together a deal with the Best company to build a smaller, cheaper version of the crawler. White was convinced that there could be a "tractor that would be the Ford Model T of the industry."

But Best was not interested in selling a smaller tractor and he was not interested in a business association with White. So White decided to build one himself. He went back to Cleveland and organized the Cleveland Plow Company which became the Cleveland Tractor Company one year later. The White brothers took their newly acquired 8-16 Best crawler to a new home in a suburb of Cleveland, Euclid, Ohio. They built a factory, organized the corporate offices and made up a sales brochure with a picture of the Best 8-16. Then they designed and built a small crawler tractor which combined the features of the Yuba Ball

It doesn't look a lot like a John Deere Model BO, but that's what's inside. This is the Lindeman-John Deere Model BO. The Lindeman Power Equipment Company started out as a tractor dealer and service agency supporting the huge apple orchards around Yakima, Washington. Wheeled tractors didn't do very well in that part of the country and crawlers were the weapon of choice. Lindeman started the conversions on a free-lance, experimental basis, pretty much to see if it was possible to cross a Deere engine and drive-train with a Best Model 30 set of tracks and undercarriage. The Lindeman-John Deere BO was the ultimate result and many are still working just as this one was over sixty years ago. *John Deere*

Bill Bechtold Sr., Oliver—Cletrac Dealer

I started working for a Cletrac dealer in 1934, and worked there for eleven years, mostly in the service department. Then Oliver bought Cletrac, so I was working on both kinds of tractors. I became shop foreman, but then, in 1949, things weren't going so well at the dealership and I quit to go farming. But folks found out I had left and they came by to ask if I'd work on their tractors. I could never say no, so I worked out of the back of the pickup and had a little shop here at my dad's place.

Then, about 1953, some people from the Oliver corporation came by to see me. They asked me if I wanted to be an Oliver dealer. I was young and didn't have much money. I told them I didn't have the money for it. They looked me in the eye and said, "Look, Bill, we didn't ask you if you had any money or not, we asked you if you wanted to be an Oliver dealer." That perked me up a little, and we talked for a while. Then we all went down to the bank and made arrangements to set up the dealership.

I was learning something completely new and it took a while to figure it out. I stocked a couple of tractors and a spraying machine. But it took a whole year to sell the first tractor. That started the ball rolling! The other one sold a month later. So we got a couple more from the branch house in Oakland, and the dealership started to grow. I got some employees and a bigger shop. We were selling crawlers.

By then they were calling them Oliver crawlers, the OC (for Oliver Crawler) Series — we sold a lot of those OC-3s, OC-4s around here, and OC-6s and OC-12s. They were all beautiful, wonderful tractors. We stayed with them after the company became White, but quit selling them when AGCO took over in the late 1970s.

I don't remember just when I got started collecting Cletrac and Oliver crawlers, but it must have been around that time. Our family settled in this area where my shop is in 1908, and farmed here with horses. Their first tractor was a Cleveland, the forerunner of the Cletrac. So I wanted to collect tractors that my family had owned over the years, starting with the Cleveland Model R. I picked up one here and there. Once you get a reputation for that, people start coming by to offer you machines. That's how I came to collect Cletracs, about sixty examples — not many duplicates and a good cross-section of the product line. I've been told that it is one of the best collections of these tractors in the country, from 1916 till the last ones. Only six or eight are missing, and I know where they are.

So now I am in the restoration business. I rebuild machines for people, as well as myself, and manufacture parts and decals for restorers. My restorations are complete, not cosmetic. We overhaul the engine and drive train so the crawler is like a new machine — you can put one to work in the field for eight or ten years when we're done. The only trouble with doing a full restoration like that is that we like to run them around in the dirt after we're done, and that gets the paint scratched.

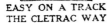

**HARD THIS
WAY, BUT—**

**EASY ON A TRACK
THE CLETRAC WAY**

SPECIFICATIONS

Horsepower:
  12 at drawbar,
  20 at belt-pulley
Length: 96 inches
Width: 50 inches
Height: 52 inches
Weight: 3420 pounds
Turning Circle: 12 feet
Traction Surface:
  About 800 square inches
*Center to Center of
  Tracks:* 38 inches
Belt Pulley: Diameter
  8 inches, face 6 inches

Cletrac Works Easily
Among the Trees

CLETRAC is low-set and smooth-bodied. It slips in and out among the trees with short quick turns. It's only 13 hands high and has no projections to catch low-hanging branches or scrape and bruise the bark.

With a Cletrac to turn under your cover crop, you can work right up close to the trees. This tractor leaves no patches of unplowed ground that so often makes orchard plowing a half-power, half-horse job.

After plowing, Cletrac follows through with discing, fertilizing and lime-crushing. Its broad tank-type treads carry Cletrac lightly over the soft orchard ground without slipping or packing.

Our Orchard Bulletin tells how Cletrac saves fruit growers money. Let us send you a copy and see your local Cletrac dealer for a demonstration.

Cletrac
TANK-TYPE TRACTOR

THE CLEVELAND TRACTOR CO.

"Largest Producers of Tank-Type Tractors in the World"

18935 Euclid Avenue   Cleveland, Ohio

Tread and the little Best. The popular little machine became famous as the "Cletrac."

While other tractor makers merged with thresher builders and implement distributors over the years, the management of Cletrac stuck with a single machine. A sales brochure written in 1941 says they have over 36,000 units of one model in service. In 1939 they affiliated with the B. F. Avery Company of Louisville, Kentucky, in order to offer a line of agricultural implements for the crawler. Both the Cleveland Tractor Company and the Avery organization were folded into the Oliver Company in 1944.

Owner Profile: Bill Bechtold Sr.

Bill Bechtold has been serving fruit growers in the Lodi, California, area for over sixty years. It is an area that's been intensively farmed for 150 years, and tree fruits and vineyards have always been important in this region. You won't see many classic wheeled tractors here—crawlers are very common, unlike in the east or cornbelt. Bill explains why:

Out here in the west the ground gets worked harder than in the midwest. And a lot of our ground is 'spotty,' with hard patches in the middle of soft ground, especially in the spring when some of the ground might be wet and others dry and hard.

And here in the Lodi area, where we have a lot of grape vines, the vineyards were laid out to be cultivated with horses, with narrow row spacing. A horse is narrow, and wheeled tractors are usually pretty wide. Crawlers were designed to fit between the vines, and the Cleveland worked fine that way; it could turn at the end of the rows, too, where there wasn't enough room for tractors back then.

Over on what we call the "west side," over by Tracy and down to Bakersfield, the ground is tough and hard. You have to have a track layer to pull a ripper or subsoiler, to loosen that compacted soil, otherwise the plants don't grow well. A crawler has much better traction for the same horsepower than a wheeled tractor. You need one to work the soil that deep.

Crawlers don't compact the soil, either, the way a wheeled tractor does. That's really a problem in the vineyards where you go right down the same ground every time. That makes "hard-pan" and keeps the water from percolating down to the roots properly.

Crawlers are more comfortable to drive, if you ask me. You don't bounce around the way you do on a regular tractor.

LEFT

Cletrac advertisement, circa 1935.

Cletrac is First in the Orchards

—it "gets the jump" when the season's late

CLETRAC is first in the orchards every year. Even a late, wet Spring doesn't bother the Cletrac fruit grower. He gets the plowing and discing cleaned up early regardless of weather. And he's ready to seed his cover crop during those few days when conditions are just right for planting.

The compact, smooth bodied Cletrac works in close to the trees without harm to bark or branches. Its sure-gripping tank-type tracks carry it easily over hilly land without losing power through slipping or digging in. It leaves the earth loose and mellow because the broad tracks don't pack the fresh-turned soil.

Cletrac jumps right into its fast, steady gait the first day out. And if the season's unusually backward, it will keep it up day and night to finish the job while the weather holds good.

"The Cletrac Orchard Bulletin" contains many valuable tractor facts. We'll gladly send it on request or you can get a copy from the Cletrac dealer near you.

THE CLEVELAND TRACTOR CO.

"Largest Producers of Tank-Type Tractors in the World"

18935 Euclid Ave.   Cleveland, Ohio

HARD THIS WAY BUT—

EASY ON A TRACK THE CLETRAC WAY

SPECIFICATIONS

Horsepower:
    12 at drawbar,
    20 at belt-pulley.
Length: 96 inches
Width: 50 inches
Height: 52 inches
Weight: 3420 pounds
Turning Circle: 12 feet
Traction Surface:
    About 800 square inches
Center to Center of Tracks: 38 inches
Belt Pulley: Diameter 8 inches, face 6 inches

Cletrac TANK-TYPE TRACTOR

Cletrac advertisement, circa 1935.

Cletrac Model AD

The little Cletrac AD demonstrated by Bill Bechtold, Jr., began life in 1937 as a gasoline-powered little crawler tractor primarily for farm and orchard use. Cletrac brought the same machine out in a diesel version, first with a Buda engine for the first four years of production and then with a Hercules power-plant. This was the first small diesel crawler on the market, with direct electric starting (instead of a "pony" gasoline engine) from the very beginning. It stayed on the market until 1959. The AD offered 30hp at the drawbar, comparable to the competitive D2 from Caterpillar.

Bill Bechtold's AD sold originally from the Stockton, California, Cletrac dealer and went to work on a farm near Lodi. Bill serviced the machine many times during its productive life. The tractor was sold to a fruit grower in the same area and when the company finally closed, the tractor came up for sale. Bill bought it to rebuild and resell as a working machine, but ended up using it to farm with instead. "I like this one because it has a higher speed second-gear, and we use second almost all the time, rather than third."

109

Caterpillar

Those funny folks in California, you know they always do things differently. They drain marsh land to grow beets and then they flood good wheat acreage to grow rice. They put orchards in the desert. So it should probably not surprise you to learn that the strange looking Caterpillar crawler tractor, that curious little machine that runs on treads rather than wheels, was first developed on the West coast. However it may surprise you to learn just how early it was first developed. Benjamin Holt built his first crawler tractor, a machine powered by a steam engine, way back in 1904.

Now that you know the machine was bred and born in California, it should not surprise you that inventor Ben Holt invited a couple of artists to his first field trial; a painter, John Shepard and a photographer, Charles Clements. Setting up his camera to take pictures of the new invention, Clements looked at the machine moving across his lens and observed that it looked like a "caterpillar." Holt liked the nickname and the tracked crawler became known as the Caterpillar.

Bill Bechtold Jr. adjusts the throttle, adding power before taxiing out for a trip around the peach patch. The Cletrac AD is a diesel-engined machine, but early crawlers were normally gas-guzzlers until well into the 1930s.

Those after-market fenders are a necessity in groves like this, where the rows are close and the growth is low. The problem is compounded at harvest time when the trees sag under the weight of the crop. Then it is quite easy for limbs to catch in the passing machine, ripping a limb right off the tree. Crawlers have the added advantage of being quite low to the ground, even without shrouding and fenders, avoiding much of the chance for snags.

The machine quickly demonstrated that it was a practical design for California's unique agricultural conditions. Thousands of acres of extremely fertile delta were too boggy for conventional steam tractors. The heavy machines sank through the marshy grassland and disappeared forever. The Caterpillar tractor was an extremely practical solution, its treads spread the weight of the machine and offered superior traction.

By mid 1915 there were three tracked crawlers on the market in California, all being used for farm operations in the Sacramento delta farmland. Historian Randy Leffingwell quotes a Caterpillar sales manager Frank Cornell about the early appearance of the tracked crawler for orchard work. "Best, Holt and Yuba were all there in a battle for

Here comes Cliff Koster on his home-brewed International Harvester orchard crawler. Cliff's family has been farming this ground since 1888 and a lot of ag history is tucked away safe and sound in his big barns. The tractor came from World War II surplus—it was a fork-lift in a previous life. Cliff adapted it to honest work and is busy discing the walnut grove to help catch the winter rains. Those discs behind him have been farming as long as Cliff, since the 1930s. The whole package seems to be going strong.

crawler supremacy." Cornell goes on to list his favorite machines. "I had the Best 75, the Best 30 'Muley' and the new 8-16. This one aimed at the orchard [owner] and small rancher was built to sell at $1,400. That little crawler was a pulling fool."

The Caterpillar crawler tractor, the most enduring of the crawler machines, was the result of a love-hate relationship between the Daniel Best Company of San Leandro, California and the Benjamin Holt Company of Stockton, California. The Best Company built a combined grain harvester and separator that had been especially modified for use on large California farms. After outgrowing several smaller locations, Best finally located all his equipment and machinery in San Leandro in 1886.

The Holt Company has a similar history. In 1883 the Holt Brothers founded the Stockton Wheel Company. They were soon repairing agricultural machinery and quickly decided that they could improve the performance of the harvesters that were being used in San Joaquin Valley. In 1886 they introduced their Improved Link Belt Combined Harvester. By 1895 they were the primary competition for the Best Company.

The two businesses were located about forty miles apart. Best specialized in steam powered traction engines; Holt built combined harvesters. Sometimes an employee of one company would quit and then go to work for the other. Engineering modifications by one company were quickly adopted by the other. The two were competitive but each seemed respectful of the other contribution to the industry. But the situation didn't last.

The two firms started butting heads when they both started to built steam powered combines. The rivalry became more intense when gasoline engines were adapted to fit agricultural machinery. The first lawsuit between Best and Holt claimed patent infringement and was filed in 1905. After considerable wrangling and time in the courtroom, the two companies turned to negotiation.

The Holt brothers bought the assets of the Best Company for $750,000 in 1908 and the companies merged. Father Daniel Best retired from business but his son, C. L. Best

The Antique Gas & Steam Engine Museum collection at Vista, California, includes many orchard tractors, including this Lindeman-John Deere Model BO.

went to work with the Holt's. The terms of the merger prevented Best from entering the tractor business for ten years. But he ignored this requirement and opened another tractor company in about 1910 called The C. L. Best Gas Traction Company.

The companies went to court again in 1925 and consolidated once more. But this time the tables were turned and the Best family and management was in charge. They fired all of the Holt's and their old-time employees, burned the company records and moved the manufacturing plant to Peoria, Illinois. So you might say that Holt and Best were like some unhappily married couples. . .they did pretty well when the companies were merged but they just couldn't live together.

Caterpillar Orchard Models

You didn't see many Cats in the east or midwest, but they were all over the west, from Washington down to the Mexican border. Richard Walker's family used them in their citrus groves in the El Toro and Irvine area of California, from the 1920's onwards. Back then most of Southern California was rural, quiet, and heavily agricultural. The warm climate and fertile soil offered excellent growing conditions where water for irrigation was available. But the soft, sandy soil and the importance of preventing hard-pan favored the crawler tractor over the wheeled version. So too did the crawler's turning ability at the end of a row, and clearly superior drawbar power. A wheeled tractor could turn with a eight or ten foot radius; a crawler would do it in its own width, a pivot turn.

Marvin Fery is the president of the Antique Caterpillar Machinery Owner's Club, a fairly new group dedicated to old Caterpillar crawlers. "Almost every tractor Caterpillar made, up through the 1940s," he says, "came in three option packages—the *standard gauge*, the *wide-gauge*, and the *orchard*. The orchard version was commonly called the "tail-seat" model because the cast iron seat position was quite low; the orchard model came with track fenders and the controls were all repositioned to be low and out of the way. You could get this package on just about anything Cat made—the Cat 10, 15, 22, even up through the 40s. One guy in our

Doug Peltzer's set of John Deere orchard models naturally includes a Lindeman-John Deere Model BO, here posing attractively among the Valencia orange trees.

Controls for the Lindeman-John Deere BO crawler.

114

Vineyard tractors need to be narrow and the Cat D2 fits nicely. Bill Garnett is disking soon after the harvest; soon all the leaves will fall as the vines begin their dormant period. Disking prepares the ground to receive rainfall; Bill's orchard gets about 20in each winter. These vines will receive no irrigation during the long growing season so good cultivation of the vineyard, percolating water deep into the ground, is an essential part of crop management.

club specializes in these, and he's got about fifty of them!"

Caterpillar Model 22

The Cat 22 came out in 1934 and lasted until 1939. Only two track gauges were availabe on the 22, 50in for the wide gauge version, 40in for the narrow-gauge. Orchard models got 10in track shoes, hoods, side panels, and fenders as standard equipment. List price was $1,595 in 1936. There were two series of Model 22 production, the 2F "early series" and the 1J "late series."

The engine design was a pretty standard four-cylinder, with overhead valves and a 4in by 5in bore and stroke. The 22 was rated at 19.3 drawbar horsepower, 27.2 on the pulley at 1,250rpm. In low the Nebraska test recorded a 4,900lb pull at 1.93mph and a slippage of 3.29 percent. The operator of the Cat 22 had a choice of three forward gears, offering up to 3.6mph, and a 2.1mph reverse. Despite its small size, the 22 tipped the scales at better than three tons, 6,210lb.

"Back in the 1950's I used to ride my bike to school down seldom-used country roads, through solid orange groves." Richard Walker recalls, "it was some of the best farming land in the country. Flat, deep loam soil and a mild climate. Everybody and his brother used Caterpillars, including our family. We used crawlers instead of wheeled tractors because in the 1930s and 1940s no wheeled tractors could compete with what you could get out of a crawler of the same horsepower. It wasn't until the 1950s that the manufacturers started offering suitable wheeled models with three-point-hitchs that could work efficiently in the groves. That is when the switch finally began in our business. Wheel tractors were also mechanically simpler and cheaper to maintain

"I like collecting Cats because of nostalgia, as much as anything, since I grew up in citrus groves where they were common. And I like them because they were built in the days when form really did follow function—they are simple, direct,over-built, and you can work on most everything yourself. All the components are accessible, even if it takes some work to get at parts of the machine. Working on the engine isn't much different than an engine on any tractor, but getting to it and the drive train can take heavy jacks, a chain hoist and a lot of work. Crawlers are

Spring chisel tools like these are important in citrus cultivation, breaking up the compacted soil between the rows. The hitch isn't original; owner Richard Walker fabricated it for this application. *Richard Walker*

Bill Garnett's Caterpillar D2 was until recently part of the Christian Brothers huge wine grape growing operation in California's fabled Napa Valley. When a new management team decided such old tractors couldn't possibly be cost-efficient, Bill grabbed one at the sale for his own smaller operation. Even though maximum drawbar horsepower is rated at a puny 25.86lb, the Cat's gearing and tractive ability turn that into 6680lb of drawbar pull in first gear, more than enough to carve up the surface of the earth pretty much anyway you want.

built for eternity, if you take care of them. As long as you inspect and grease it daily, change the oil on time, maintain the machine as was intended, you get a lot of years out of a Caterpillar. I'm not one of those collectors who likes putting a machine in absolutely perfect show condition; instead, I like finding an old Cat that hasn't run for a long time and is headed for the scrap heap, paying a few hundred bucks for it, and getting it running and functional again. That's what I enjoy, and that's how I collect tractors," said Walker

The resale market for Cats is pretty good, at least in the west where farmers are used to them and a support network of aftermarket parts dealers sell components. Today, any rusty Cat in barely running condition is worth from $1,000 and up to a collector or to somebody who needs to put it to work. Restored antique crawlers in excellent mechanical condition can

fetch thousands of dollars. And there is no age discrimination when it comes to Cats in the agricultural west where fifty-year-old machines can still be found doing the same job for which they were hired when new.

Bill Garnett's D2

One of those is an elderly but pristine and vigorous D2 owned by Bill Garnett of Napa, California. Bill's Cat came from the huge vineyards of the Christian Brothers winery in the Napa Valley, one of a litter of eleven D2s used by the operation for almost fifty years. For many years the winery was run by Brother Timothy, an able administrator. During his tenure, two of the Cats received a complete overhaul each year, bringing them up to virtually new condition.

But when he retired a few years ago a new team took over. The new team looked at

The Lindeman Connection

Some of the D models went to the Lindeman Power Equipment Company in Yakima, Washington, for conversion to crawler tractors. The Lindeman outfit had been just another dealer for the crawler tractors so popular in the West and Northwest—the Holt and Best at first, then Cletrac later, followed by John Deere in 1930. The Model D made a big hit with the Lindemans who liked everything about it, except for those tall, pesky wheels. Jesse Lindeman figured the D had the makings of a good crawler, so he dug around out in the shop and came up with an old set of rollers and tracks from a Best 30 track-type tractor. With a good bit of tinkering the conversion worked well enough to try in the field, and some went to work the many large orchards near Yakima. Although the steering was rather goofy—you had to use track braking to turn—the experiment was a huge success and orchard owners clamored for more. They were to get them, but not based on the Model D foundation. The Deere records call these early experimental tractors Lindeman - John Deere D With Crawler Attachment. *Jack Cherry observes, "I think Lindeman probably had some intent for these to work in orchards although there isn't any hint of it in the photographs. Lindeman did the testing of these tractors on flat ground and was looking for increased pulling power—and didn't get it with this machine. It was a bigger tractor than is needed in an orchard."*

the books and found 11 tractors that seemed to be hopelessly ancient, obsolete, and presumably worn out. Over the protests of the vineyard manager, the new management team decided to sell off the old Cats in favor of new tractors.

Bill's acreage is tiny by comparison to some of the big operations in the valley, but he still needed another crawler to help with his first machine, a Lindeman-John Deere BO. The Christian Brother's fleet appeared for sale in the paper. Bill consulted his tractor mechanic, a man who had done all the major overhauls on these D2s, and asked his advice. "Numbers 129 and 130 have the freshest overhauls," he said. The price tag on 130 was $9,000 and 129 was $8,500; Bill took 129. "It seemed like plenty of money," Bill says, "but considering their condition, I think they were worth it."

Bill's wife, Eula, made him new cushions for the seat and back for Christmas, and they come in the house on the rare occasions when the tractor stays out in the vineyard overnight. The tractor gets a tarp over it. This is probably one of the most pampered iron kitties of all time.

"My tractor looks bigger than a standard D2," Bill says, "it sits higher off the ground because they put oversized idler wheels on them, and it has a wide gauge and wide tracks so it is good on our hills. I had a hydraulic cylinder installed for the disc, and converted the starting system from the original "pony" engine to electric start.

"One of the most curious things about my D2 was discovered when I started having a problem with the Bendix starter. Somehow, the ring gear had been installed backwards during one of the overhauls and the pinion was barely engaging." Well, they fixed that, but getting at the engine in any Cat is major surgery. It starts fine now, and here's how Bill does it:

"Because it used to have a pony engine for starting, the tractor still has a compression release. I like to use it because I figure it reduces the strain on the electrical starter, although it will start without that release. Then you turn the master switch to ON, energizing the electrical system. Then the throttle is advanced past the idle detent, to about one-third throttle. Then you hit the starter, and after a revolution or two, it fires. I like to help things along with a little squirt of starting fluid when it is dead cold—there aren't any glow plugs so it starts strictly by compression."

Lindeman-John Deere

John Deere's little Lindeman crawler is just about as cute as any baby bulldozer ever gets. A lot of folks thought so, too, because it sold by the thousands, especially to western fruit growers. Its low-slung, muscular lines disguise what is really a standard Deere Model B tractor that's been lowered, customized, and converted to run on tracks.

The Lindeman conversion was the brainchild of Jesse Lindeman, a former Cletrac dealer who noticed that the standard Model D tractor was an almost perfect candidate to accept crawler tracks. The first conversion used a set of spare Best tracks in the back of the dealership.

The Lindeman Power Equipment Company and Deere had a long relationship, based on that first conversion. The BO crawler—seldom called by its proper name—is listed by Deere as the Lindeman–John Deere BO. Production began in 1939, converting up to twenty-five B tractors a week at the Yakima, Washington, factory. The run lasted for 1,675 units, ending in 1947.

There are still a lot of Lindemans around, and some still work for a living. Bill Garnett owns one and uses it in his vineyard where its diminutive size is a perfect fit. Doug Peltzer owns one, too, but more for show than go.

"One reason you find most Lindemans in the west," Doug says, "is that a lot went to hilly little orchard operations in Northern California, Oregon, and Washington—five and ten acre orchards in apples, walnuts, or pears. These hillside orchards are just too steep for a wheeled tractor, it would roll over on you."

Here's Richard's Cat 22 after a couple of years of hard work and heavy lifting, back in the dirt. *Richard Walker*

1936 Caterpillar 22 fresh from the sale. Richard Walker found this one at an auction in 1985, neglected and unloved, and it followed him home. Richard likes to use the tractors in his collection, rather than have them glitter in showroom-fresh condition, so the 22 was brought back to life and put to work. Part of the project involved an elaborate hydraulic hitch fabrication that adapted the old crawler to modern tillage tools—and won Richard a $2,000 prize from the James F. Lincoln Arc Welding Foundation. *Richard Walker*

NEXT PAGE
A Lindemann—John Deere Model BO works the orchard floor of a Washington state fruit farm sometime during the 1940s. *John Deere*

APPENDIX

Richard Walker Explains
Citrus Cultivation Implements

Richard Walker describes the detailed process of Southern California citrus cultivation before 1960. Richard's family has been in the citrus business for about 80 years and has owned and operated all sorts of orchard tractors. The Walker clan even once owned one of those mythical John Deere "California Special" versions of the Waterloo Boy – but unfortunately sent it off to the scrap dealer long ago. Their groves were in Orange, Irvine and El Toro, in the Orange County area, south of Los Angeles.

Terminology

The ongoing cycle of citrus grove care when a grove was under cultivation was disc, furrow out, irrigate—disc, furrow out, irrigate—and so on, right up until the rainy season started, usually in December. Then you'd let the weeds grow over the winter and disc down a TALL growth of weeds in the early spring, when the cycle would commence all over again. Irrigation frequency was dependent upon soil type. Light sandy loams would require water once every week to ten days. Heavy clay soils could last four or five weeks between irrigations.

Disc:

Three-point hitch lift-up discs were considered too light to really be effective in the orchards of Orange County. Most all citrus growers around me used heavy drag discs, hitched to the drawbar of an orchard crawler. Discs almost always were offset models (two gangs, one behind the other, using 18 to 22in blades) usually in the 5 to 6ft width range. Typically orchard discs were fitted with a contoured sheet steel shield over the top, to slide under the tree canopy and avoid injury to the limbs as well as minimizing fruit scarring. You'd set up the hitch so the disc would run a foot or so to the side of your tractor, and thus be able to get back under the limb canopy better.

The older discs (pre-1950s) were rope-operated to open and close the gangs for transport; you'd need to back the tractor and disc up while tugging on the rope to close and lock the gangs straight. Later discs used a hydraulic cylinder plugged into the tractor hydraulics to angle the gangs. Some orchard discs were fitted with depth control wheels to allow for setting the depth of cut precisely. It was also quite common to adjust the depth of cut for non-wheel drag discs by adding weight to the disc frame. Old railroad rails or concrete blocks were often used. You wanted enough weight so the disc would turn under an average amount of weed growth readily, but not so much that it would cut too deeply. Deep discing damaged roots of the surface-rooted citrus trees, plus took more tractor horsepower. Most orchard discs were equipped with blade cleaner scrapers for each blade, to avoid clogging with wet soil. Using a disc behind an orchard crawler, doing three passes down each row lengthwise and two passes crosswise, you could disc ten to fifteen acres a day.

Spring tooth harrow:

Spring tooths were used for the same purposes as discs, but limited to soil with only a light growth of weeds. Too high a growth and the spring tooth would clog. Too wet, heavy soil and it wouldn't work well either. Growers typically used a three bar harrow, with about a 6 or 7ft width. Spring tooths often were fitted with sheet steel covers, like discs. It was common to use a disc to turn under the winter weed growth in the early spring, then employ a spring tooth the rest of the year. Given the right conditions, a spring tooth was great for cultivating after an irrigation, knocking the old furrows down and getting the soil loose for the next furrowing.

Furrowers:

Two types were commonly used, shovel and disc. Shovel furrowers used middle-buster bottoms (usually three or four) on a sled-type frame (for drag operation behind a Cat) or attached to a 3-point tool carrier (for 3-point hitch operation behind a wheel tractor). Shovel furrowers were quick and easy to use, provided the soil was freshly disced, loose, and mostly free of trash (old weeds). Two fast passes per row middle, up and back, and that was it. They didn't take much horsepower to pull. We'd use a Cat for discing and a Ford 8-N for the furrowing. Early Fords were excellent for furrowing, fast and maneuverable, but lacked the weight and horsepower for orchard discing. The advent of Ford wheel tractors meant more and more growers started using shovel furrowers past 1950.

Disc furrowers were used fairly universally around here back in the 1920s to late 1940s. Two in-line blades per furrow, one angled in, the other out, usually a three-furrow model, equipped with depth wheels to control the depth of the cut and also to raise the furrower out of the ground when turning at the end of rows. You'd tug one rope to raise the furrower (a set of ratchets on the wheels would catch a pawl, raising the unit), and another rope to drop it back down again. Like discs, many disc furrowers were fitted with contoured sheet steel covers to shield the trees. A heavy disc furrower would work great in soil that had a lot of weed growth, just cutting right through all the trash. Using a disc furrower behind a Cat, you could furrow 20 to 30 acres daily.

Coil Shank Chisel:

Coil shank chisels were not regularly used. But sometimes you had to deep-cultivate an orchard to break up any hardpan layer that was forming. It was a trade-off whether you wanted to risk the inevitable root damage in return for shattering the hardpan. The springy steel shanks, each fitted with a replaceable wear point, would run 10 to 15 inches deep through the soil, flexing back and forth to thoroughly shatter any hardpan present. The shanks were mounted on a field cultivator frame, usually with wheels, and it took the power of a crawler to pull this implement.

Then of course there were more esoteric grove implements, like weed and grass knives, spike tooth harrows, railroad tie drags, smudge pot sleds, checker/blocker attachments for furrowers, and more.

Tractor Specifications

International Harvester

IH Orchard Models, 1949 specs	O-4	O-6	ODS-6
Maximum Belt HP, Gasoline	27.5	38.5	
Maximum Belt HP, Distillate	24	36	
Maximum Belt HP, Diesel			36
Maximum Drawbar HP, Gasoline	25	33.5	
Maximum Drawbar HP, Distillate	22	32	
Maximum Drawbar HP, Diesel			31
Speeds, mph			
First Gear	1.5	1.5	1.5
Second Gear	3.1	3.1	3.1
Third Gear	4	4	4
Fourth Gear	5	5	5
Fifth Gear	14.6	14.6	14.6
Sixth Gear			
Reverse	1.75	1.75	1.75
Belt Pulley			
Diameter And Face	9.75x7.5	11x7.5	11x7.5
rpm	1019	899	899
Belt Speed	2601	2588	2588
Power Take Off (Engine Driven)	540	537	537
Engine			
Displacement	152.1	247.7	247.7
Speed (rpm)	1650	1450	1450
Bore And Stroke (inches)	3.4x4.25	3.8x5.25	3.8x5.25
Governor	1000-1650	950-1450	800-1450
Lubrication (quarts)	6	8	13
Fuel Tank Capacity (US Gallons)			
Gasoline Engine	17.5	21	20.5
All-Fuel Engine	17.5	21	20.5
LP-Gas Engine	17.5	21	20.5
Water Capacity	4.25	6.25	21
Clutch (Hand Operated) inches	10	11	11
Rear Tires And Wheels	12-26	13-26	13-26
Front Tires	5.50-16	6.00-16	6.00-16
Rear Wheel Tread	41.75	45	45
Front Wheel Tread	46	46.75	46.75
Turning Radius	11	12.75	12.75

Drawbar Dimensions			
Overall Width	60.25	65	59.75
Overall Length	120.8	133.25	133.25
Overall Height	57.1	61.5	61.5
Wheelbase	66.75	76.25	76.25
Shipping Weight			
Gas	4320	5435	5540

O-12 Specifications (from M-D Brochure, 1934)

Rated engine horsepower	17
Number of Cylinders	4
speed of engine, rpm	1400-2000
bore of cylinders	3in
stroke of pistons	4in
pulley speed, rpm (@1400rpm)	748
Belt speed, feet per minute (@1400rpm)	2593
belt pulley diameter	13.25in
belt pulley face	6.25in
power take off, rpm (@1400rpm) 538	
speeds forward, mph (@1400rpm)	2.5, 4.5, 7.25
reverse, mph (@1400rpm)	2.5
speeds forward, mph (@2000rpm)	3.5, 6, 10.5
reverse, mph (@2000rpm)	3.5
front wheels (low pressure tires)	6.00 x 9 (21.5in OD)
rear wheels (low pressure tires)	9.00 x 24 (42.5in OD)
turning radius	8.5ft
tread, front	39.5in
tread, rear	40.5
wheelbase	60in
length overall	103in
height of steering wheel	52in
capacity of fuel tank	11gal
drawbar adjustment, vertical	4.5in
drawbar adjustment, lateral	25.5in
approximate shipping weight	3200lb

Case model VAO 1942, 1945-1955 Specs

Wheelbase	75.25 in.
Front Wheel Tread	43in (early units); 58.25in (late units)
Rear Wheel Tread	44-72in (early units); 48-72in (late units with shell fenders); 52in with crown fenders.
Standard	Shell type fenders; cushioned seat
Options	Orchard crown rear wheel fenders; orchard shield and cowl attachments; rear fender closures; PTO; belt pulley; Eagle Hitch w/hydraulic lift (from 1949); electric starter (standard from 1948) and lights (standard from 1952); Low Cost Fuel (from 1947).
Length	121in with fenders and platform
Height	49.5in at radiator cap; 54.75in to top of fenders; 54.75 to top of steering wheel
Wheelbase	74.25in
Shipping Weight	4135lb with 4in lugs, no fuel or water

John Deere Model GPO Specifications (from 1931 brochure)

Power	Suitable for two 14in plows or 22in thresher or 24in John Deere thresher
Speeds, mph	
First Gear	2.25mph
Second Gear	3mph
Third Gear	4mph
Reverse	1.75mph
Belt Pulley	
Diameter And Face	13in diameter, 6.5in face
rpm	950
Belt Speed	3200fpm
Power Take Off (Engine Driven)	for front or rear connections rotates clockwise, 520rpm; separate gear shift
Engine	
Speed (RPM)	950
Bore And Stroke	6in x 6in
Governor	enclosed fly-ball type
Carburation	double nozzle type with air choker
Ignition	high tension magneto, with enclosed impulse starter
Lubrication	force feed, geared pump
Cooling	tubular radiator, thermosiphon
Electrical System	
Lighting	
Fuel Tank Capacity (US Gallons)	
Gasoline	2gal
Distillate or Kerosene	16gal
Water Capacity	9gal
Clutch (Hand Operated)	10in dry discs, locking in and out
Rear Tires And Wheels	steel
Front Tires	
Rear Wheel Tread	49.5in
Front Wheel Tread	
Turning Radius	8
Drawbar	adjustable up and down 4.5in, lateral 34.5in
Dimensions	
Overall Width	64in with orchard fenders

John Deere Model A Specifications (early model–later versions quite different)

Power	rated to pull load equivalent to six horses or mules; will operate 24in John Deere thresher
	18.7hp, 24.7hp Drawbar /Belt or PTO (early engine)
	26.2 - 29.6hp Drawbar /Belt or PTO (distillate)
	34.1-38hp Drawbar /Belt or PTO (gasoline)
Displacement	309ci (early engines) 321 (late engines)
Speeds, mph	
First Gear	2mph
Second Gear	3mph
Third Gear	4mph
Fourth Gear	6.25mph
Reverse	3mph
Belt Pulley	
Diameter And Face	12.75x4.25in
Rpm	975
Belt Speed	3270
Power Take Off (Engine Driven)	544rpm
Engine	
Speed (rpm)	975rpm
Bore And Stroke	5.5x6.5in
Governor	John Deere design enclosed fly-ball type with one ball thrust and two self-adjusting ball bearings
Carburation	Natural draft type with load and thrust adjustments
Ignition	high tension magneto with enclosed automatic impulse starter
Lubrication	Full force feed pressure system with oil filter
Cooling	thermo siphon with gear and shaft-driven fan (no belts or water pump)
Electrical System	none
Lighting	none
Fuel Tank Capacity (US Gallons)	
Gasoline Engine	
All-Fuel Engine	16gal kerosene, 1gal gasoline (for starting)
LP-Gas Engine	
Water Capacity	8gal
Clutch (Hand Operated)	two 10in dry discs – locking in and out
Rear Tires And Wheels	Orchard model: 42.75in diameter, 10in face
Front Tires	28in diameter, 6in face
Rear Wheel Tread	50.5in
Wheelbase	76in

Turning Radius	13ft steering only; 9ft 10.5in using differential braking
Drawbar	12in/14in/16in vertical adjustment
26.5in horizontal adjustment	
Dimensions	
Overall Width	61in
Length	124in
Height	55in
Wheelbase	
Shipping Weight	4088lb
Gas	
LP Gas	

John Deere Model 620

Power	Four plow – not tested at Nebraska
Speeds, mph	14-26 low profile tires
First Gear	1.5
Second Gear	2.5
Third Gear	3.5
Fourth Gear	4.25
Fifth Gear	6.25
Sixth Gear	10.7
Reverse	2.75
Belt Pulley	
Diameter And Face	12-13/16in x 7 3/8in
rpm	1125
Belt Speed - Feet Per Minute	3775
Power Take Off (Engine Driven)	540
Engine	
Speed (rpm)	1125
Bore And Stroke	5 x 6 3/8in
Governor	enclosed fly ball type with one ball-thrust and two self adjusting ball bearings
Carburation	dual induction with double barrel carburetor and individually ported valves
Ignition	camshaft driven, automotive-type distributor
Lubrication	force-feed pressure system with full flow oil filter
Cooling	bypass cooling system with centrifugal pump and heavy duty thermostat
Electrical System	12-volt system with voltage regulator. Cigarette lighter available on all models
Lighting	two front lights and one rear combination white and red warning light
Fuel Tank Capacity (US Gallons)	
Gasoline Engine	20 gal
All-Fuel Engine	20 gal plus one gallon gasoline
LP-Gas Engine	total volume 38gal (fill to 85%)
Water Capacity	7gal
Clutch (Hand Operated)	four 10in dry discs

Rear Tires And Wheels	14-26 6-ply tires mounted on cast wheels recommended for average field conditions
13-26 6 ply and 14-26 6 ply low profile tires available as special equipment	
Front Tires	6.00-16 4 ply and 7.50-16 4 ply
Rear Wheel Tread	55 7/16in or 63 7/16in
Front Wheel Tread	47 3/4in
Turning Radius	13ft 8in
Drawbar	conforms to ASAE-SAE standard for drawbar hitch location
Dimensions	
Overall Width	77 5/8in
Length	125 7/8in
Height	59in
Wheelbase	75 3/4in
Shipping Weight	
Gas	6345lb
LP Gas	6645lb

1931 Case Model C Specs:

Rated Brake Horsepower	27
Rated Drawbar Horsepower	17
Cylinder	Four; bore, 3 7/8in; stroke, 5in
Normal Engine Speed	1100rpm
Ignition	Bosch mag w/impulse coupling
Carb	Kingston vertical w/single nozzle
Fuel Capacity	Gas, 2gal; kerosene, 18 gal
Cooling System	Capacity, 5 gal
Road Speed	Equipped w/ standard steel wheels; 2 1/3, 3 1/3, 4mph; Equipped w/ rubber tires; 2, 3 1/3, 5mph
Wheelbase	66in
Height to top of hood	48in
Outside turning radius	10ft
Front wheels	Diameter, 28in; width, 5in
Rear Wheels	Diameter, 42in; width, 12in

Case DO–1940 Specs.

Rated Brake HP:	31.87 (per model D)
Rated Drawbar HP:	24.86 (per model D)
Cylinder	Four: bore, 3 7/8in, stroke 5in
Norm. engine speed	1100rpm
Ignition	Case mag w/ impulse coupling
Carb	Zenith 62Axj9
Fuel Cap. Gas,.	17 gal
Cooling system	Cap, 6gal
Road Speed	(on rubber) 1, 3 , 4 2/3, 9 1/3mph
Turning Radius	10ft.
Front Wheels	6:00x16 rubber
Rear Wheels	11:25.24 rubber
Height to top of hood	55in (rubber)
Wheelbase	66 3/8in
Rear wheel tread	50in
Overall Width	62in

Overall Length	116in
Total production	1939-1952 2,874 units
Total production of DOVS (vineyard special)	582 units

John Deere Model BO Specifications:

Power	
Speeds, mph	
First Gear	2
Second Gear	3
Third Gear	4
Fourth Gear	6.25
Fifth Gear	
Sixth Gear	
Reverse	3
Belt Pulley	
Diameter And Face	10.6in x 5.5in
rpm	1150
Belt Speed	3200fpm
Power Take Off (Engine Driven)	553
Engine	
Speed (rpm)	1150
Bore And Stroke	4.5x5.5in
Governor	
Carburation	
Ignition	
Lubrication	
Cooling	
Electrical System	
Lighting	
Fuel Tank Capacity (US Gallons)	
Gasoline Engine	
All-Fuel Engine	12gal distillate, 1gal gasoline for starting
LP-Gas Engine	
Water Capacity	5.5gal
Clutch (Hand Operated)	two 8in dry discs, locking in and out
Rear Tires And Wheels	40x8in
Front Tires	24x5in
Rear Wheel Tread	42.25in
Front Wheel Tread	
Turning Radius	11ft 8in/8ft 8in with differential braking
Drawbar	12/14/16in vertical, 25.75 horizontal
Dimensions	
Overall Width	50in
Length	117.in75
Height	50.5in
Wheelbase	68in
Shipping Weight	
Gas	2870lb
LP Gas	

John Deere Model 60 Specifications (from 1953 brochure)

Power	four plow capacity
Speeds, mph	
First Gear	1.5
Second Gear	2.5
Third Gear	3.5
Fourth Gear	4.25
Fifth Gear	6.25
Sixth Gear	1.75
Reverse	2.75
Belt Pulley	
Diameter And Face	12 13/16th in x 7 3/8in
rpm	1125
Belt Speed	3775
Power Take Off (Engine Driven)	540rpm
Engine	
Speed (rpm)	1125
Bore And Stroke	5 x 7 3/8in
Governor	enclosed fly-ball type with one ball thrust and two self adjusting ball bearings
Carburation	dual induction with double barrel carburetor and individually ported valves
Ignition	camshaft driven, automotive type distributor
Lubrication	force feed pressure systems with full flow oil filter
Cooling	by pass cooling system with centrifugal pump and heavy duty thermostat
Electrical System	12 volt system with voltage regulator. Cigarette lighter available on all models
Lighting	two front lights and one rear combination white and red warning light
Fuel Tank Capacity (US Gallons)	
Gasoline Engine	20 gal
All-Fuel Engine	20 gal plus 1 gal gasoline
LP-Gas Engine	total volume 38gal (fill to 85%)
Water Capacity	7 gal
Clutch (Hand Operated)	four 10in dry discs
Rear Tires And Wheels	14-26, 6ply tires, mounted on cast wheels, recommended for average field conditions
Front Tires	6.00-16, 4 ply and 7.50-16, 4 ply
Rear Wheel Tread	55 7/16in or 63 7/16in
Front Wheel Tread	47 3/4in
Turning Radius	13ft 8in
Drawbar	conforms to ASAE-SAE standard for drawbar hitch location
Dimensions	
Overall Width	77 5/8in
Length	125 7/8in
Height	59 1/2in
Wheelbase	75 3/4in
Shipping Weight	
Gas	6345lb
LP Gas	6645lb

CLUBS, ORGANIZATIONS, AND PUBLICATIONS

All tractor brands except perhaps Kubota and Belarus have fan clubs. Some are large, others small, all are fun. Most publish excellent magazines, some of which are listed below. Everybody seems to like Pat Ertl's ANTIQUE POWER magazine, too, which covers them all in color and with good humor.

9N-2N-8N Newsletter
P.O. Box 235
Chelsea, VT 05038-0235
Gerard W. Rinaldi, Publisher
"For Ford enthusiasts"

Antique Power
Box 562
Yellow Springs, OH 45387
Pat Ertl (Publisher/Editor)
6 issues/year
$20.00 subscription. Free classifies to subscribers
1 (800) 767 5828
"All Brands Tractor Magazine"

The Belt Pulley
Box 83
Nokomis, IL 62075
6 issues/year
$16
"All Brands Tractor Magazine"

Canadian Antique Power
PO Box 120,
Teeswater ON N0G 2So
519-392-6733
ISSN 1198-5011
Published six times a year. Subscriptions $24.56CDN to Canadian addresses,
$25.00US to United States, $35.00US to foreign addresses.
"Your information source for Canadian Agricultural Antique Equipment"

Cockshutt Quarterly
International Cockshutt Club
Diana Myers
2910 Essex Road
LaRue, Ohio 43332-8830
subscription and membership: $15.00/year
"For Cockshutt, Co-op, Blackhawk, and Gambles Farmcrest enthusiasts"

The Empire Newsletter
Carl Hering
RD 1, Box 921
Cayuga, NY 13034
Twice yearly
Free (small donations accepted to help defray costs)
"For Empire tractor enthusiasts"

Engineers and Engines
P.O. Box 2757
Joliet, IL 60434-2757
6 issues/year
$15
"All brands, emphasis on steam engines"

The Ferguson Journal
Denehurst Rosehill Road
Stoke Heath
Market Drayton TF9 2JU
UNITED KINGDOM
"For Massey Ferguson enthusiasts."

Gas Engine Magazine
P.O. Box 328
Lancaster, PA 17608
12 issues/year
$27.00/in the U.S., $30.00 international.
"For enthusiasts and collectors of all types of gas engines."

The Golden Arrow
John Kasmiski
N7209 State Highway 67
Mayville, WI 53050
subscription: $16.00/year
"For Cockshutt, Co-op, Blackhawk, and Gambles Farmcrest enthusiasts"

The Golden Arrow
John Kasmiski
N7209 State Highway 67
Mayville, WI 53050
subscription: $16.00/year
"For Cockshutt, Co-op, Blackhawk, and Gambles Farmcrest enthusiasts"

Green Magazine
RR 1, Box 7
Bee, NE 68314
12 issues/year
$23.00 US, $27 foreign (in U.S. funds)
"For John Deere enthusiasts"

MM Corresponder
Rt. 1, Box 153
Vail, IA 51465
4 issues/year
$13
"For Minneapolis-Moline enthusiasts"

Old Abe's News
4004 Coal Valley Rd.
Vinton, OH 45686
4 issues/year
$20
"For Case enthusiasts"

The Old Allis News
Pleasant Knoll 10925 Love Rd.
Bellevue, MI 49021
4 issues/year
$12
"For Allis Chalmers enthusiasts"

Oliver Collector's News
Manvel, ND 58256-0044
"For Oliver enthusiasts"

Polk's
72435 SR 15
New Paris, IN 46553
6 issues/year
$18
"All Brands Tractor Magazine"

The Prairie Gold Rush
Rt. 1, Box 119
Francesville, IN 47946
4 issues/year
$15
"For Minneapolis-Moline enthusiasts"

Red Power Newsletter
Box 277
Battle Creek, IA 51006
Editor and Publisher: Daryl A. Miller
6 issues/year; start Jan
$12, $18/year Canada (US funds) Free 20 word classified ad with subscription
712-365-4669 (7pm to 10 pm) Sample copy: $2
"For All IHC(Farmall) enthusiasts"

The Rumley Newsletter
P.O. Box 12
Moline, IL 61265
For Rumley enthusiasts

Rusty Iron Monthly
Box 342
Sandwich, IL 60548
$12 /year US
$20 /year Canada
$28 /year overseas (air mail)
"All Brands Tractor Magazine"

Tractor Digest
P.O. Box 31
Eldora, IA 50627-0031
One year subscription (4 issues) $28
Two year subscription (8 issues) $50
"For John Deere enthusiasts"

Two-Cylinder Club
310 East G Avenue
Grundy Center, IA 50638
Annual Membership includes magazine - $24.00 US
"For John Deere enthusiasts"

Turtle River Toy News
Rt. 1
Manvel, ND 58256
12 issues
$16
"For Oliver enthusiasts"

Wild Harvest: Massey Collectors' News
Box 529
Denver, IA 50622
Keith Oltrogge (Publisher/Editor)
$20 subscription, second class mail. Free classifieds to members
(319) 984-5292 days, (319) 352-5524 evenings
"For Massey, Massy-Harris, and Wallis enthusiasts"

Caterpillar

The **Antique Caterpillar Machinery Owner's Club** is the organization dedicated to preserving Cat heritage and machinery. Founded in 1991, it is one of the newer organizations dedicated to old iron, but a great source of information on Cat crawlers. Membership includes a quarterly newsletter, and dues are $20 per year at this writing. Contact: Membership Secretary, Antique Caterpillar Machinery Owner's Club, 10816 Monitor McKee Road N. E., Woodburn, OR 97071.

Index

Best crawler 8 16, 107

C.L. Best Gas Traction Company, 114
Case 10-18, 53
Case 400 Orchard Diesel (Case 402), 59-61
Case 400 Orchard-LPG—"The Pound Special", 62
Case 630 Orchard (634), 62
Case 700 (715B)/730 Diesel, 62
Case Model CO, 54, 55, 57
Case Model CO Vineyard Special, 57
Case Model DO, 57, 61
Caterpillar D2, 116, 118
Caterpillar Model 22, 115
Caterpillar Orchard Models, 114
Caterpillars, 103, 110, 112
Cletracs, 106, 107

Dan Best Company, 112

Froelich, John, 29

Hart-Parr and Oliver, 71
Hart-Parr, 32
Holt Company, 112
Holt Manufacturing Company, 34
Holts, 103

International Harvester Company, 80-82

J.I. Case, 52
John Deere 2750, 15
John Deere AO, 9
John Deere Model 60 Orchard, 50, 51
John Deere Model 620, 52
John Deere Model A, 46
John Deere Model AO, 46, 47
John Deere Model B Tractor, 46, 48
John Deere Model BO, 49
John Deere Model D, 43
John Deere Model GP, 43-45
John Deere GPO, 44, 45
John Deere Waterloo Boy, 39, 41, 42

Lindeman-John Deere, 118

Massey-Harris Model 44 Orchard, 65, 69-71
McCormick, Cyrus, 81
McCormick-Deering 10-20, 80, 82, 86
McCormick-Deering Grove Tractor Model 0-14, 85
McCormick-Deering Orchard, 85
McCormick-Deering OS-4 (Orchard Special), 88, 90

Oliver, 70-72, 75, 78
Oliver 70 Orchard, 80

The Hart-Parr Company, 72
The Oliver Company, 74

Waterloo Gasoline Traction Engine Company, 29